THIS IS OUR MASS

THIS IS OUR MASS

Tom Coyle

Collins

Collins Liturgical Publications
187 Piccadilly, London W1V 9DA

First published 1982
Reprinted 1983
© 1982 Tom Coyle
ISBN 0 00 599700 3

Acknowledgements
Excerpts from the English translation of the *Rite of Baptism for Children* © 1969,
International Committee on English in the Liturgy, Inc. (ICEL); excerpts from
the English translation of *The Roman Missal* © 1973, ICEL; excerpts from the
English translation of *Eucharistic Prayers for Masses with Children* © 1975, ICEL;
patristic reading from the English translation of *The Liturgy of the Hours* © 1974,
ICEL; all rights reserved
    Excerpts from the psalms from *The Psalms a new translation*, © The Grail
(England) 1963, published by Collins

    Scripture quotations are from *Jerusalem Bible* © 1966, 1967, 1968 Darton,
Longman and Todd and Doubleday and Co Inc; and from *Good News Bible* ©
American Bible Society 1966, 1971 and 4th edition 1976

Photo credits
Brunnings, Liverpool 8, 22, 78, 128; Catholic Pictorial, Liverpool 116;
R Chapman 45; Brian McEvoy 136; Noeline Kelly 3; Carlos Reyes 70, 102;
St Joseph's Centre, Hendon 31

Typesetting by Rowland Phototypesetting Ltd
Bury St Edmunds, Suffolk
Made and printed in Great Britain by
William Collins Sons & Co Ltd

Contents

Part Five: TO LOVE AND SERVE THE LORD
The Mass in our Lives

To my wife, Marilyn
for all her help over the years

Whoever loves is a child of God and knows God.

1 John 4:7

Part One

COMING TOGETHER
The Introductory Rites

CHAPTER 1

To worship means to love

Two people meet; they get to know each other; they fall in love; they decide to get married and then, before their friends and before God, they stand and declare their love. Although our present marriage rite doesn't include it, this was one way of declaring that love:

With this ring I thee wed; with my body I thee worship;
and with all my worldly goods I thee endow.

To worship is to love; to love someone so much that we are willing to do anything for that person; to love that person because of his or her qualities of beauty or kindness or gentleness or generosity or strength or leadership. Worship, like love, tends to be blind to the failings of the loved one, seeking only the good.

We all need someone to worship. There is in all of us an instinct which tells us that there is someone or something greater than us. For primitive peoples it was the sun or the moon, or the various gods of war, harvest, fertility, and so on. In addition to the God of Christian or Jew, the great world religions – the Buddhists, the Hindus, the Muslims – all worship God under different names.

Nowadays, when many no longer believe in any god at all, some people worship the new gods of pop or film stars to fill the void. Thus when John Lennon was gunned down in a New York street, the site of the shooting was soon transformed into a shrine by his fans who brought flowers and photographs, keeping silent vigil there. The Sunday Times in a special article, 'The Dream is over', wrote:

The 25-year-old security guard who flew from Hawaii to New York with a bunch of Beatles tapes and a .38 Smith and Wesson achieved his ambition: his shots were heard around the world. The killing of John Lennon made such an impact that, for once, the globe really did feel like a village, shaken to its core by the death of a loved one.

How could a pop singer, even one who had been to the Palace, be thought so important that his murder is already compared with the assassination of a President? Why did young and old alike stop for a moment that Tuesday morning, later to be told that they would remember the very instant – where they were, what they were doing, how they heard about it – for as long as they lived?

The Beatles certainly inspired worship. Those of us who were around at the time of their greatest hits can vividly remember the newsreel films of screaming, hysterical girls welcoming them at airports or screaming at concerts, happy only to be in the same building as their heroes.

Older generations will remember the mass hysteria which surrounded the funeral of Rudolf Valentino, the great star of the silent movies; or the stunning impact of the assassination of President John F Kennedy who seemed to epitomise all that was good in modern society.

Yes, we all need someone to worship, and for many centuries in this country we were happy to worship God. Each Sunday, people would come to church to praise God and to pray to him for their needs. There is no doubt that for some, particularly in Victorian times, the motive for going to church was more social than religious, but for many, the worship of God was at the centre of their lives.

Today when the worship of God is the exception rather than the rule in our country, we need to ask ourselves whether all the others are right and we who still go out to church on a Sunday morning are wrong. Why worship God?

First of all, we believe that God exists and that God cares for us. This is a matter of faith and we have to be prepared to accept the fact of a God who actually knows and loves us; a God who created the world and all the universe; not some impersonal being but a person who has always existed and who will always exist.

One of the psalms expresses this beautifully:

> How great is your name, O Lord our God,
> through all the earth.
> When I see the heavens, the work of your hands,
> the moon and the stars which you arranged,
> what is man that you should keep him in mind,
> mortal man that you care for him. (Psalm 8)

When we go out on a starry night and look up at the stars, at the immensity of the universe, we must feel that way, and must wonder how the creator of all that could know us and want us to know him.

But he does. He wants this so much that he sent his Son, Jesus, to live on this earth to teach his followers how to know and love God, and to help them to realise that this great God is their Father. Jesus showed his followers how great is his love for them by dying the cruel and painful death on the cross. Much more, however: he showed us that death is not the end of everything by rising from the dead on Easter Day and, later, sending his Holy Spirit to share with us a new kind of life, a life without end, in which death is only a stepping stone, a short journey from our life on earth to life with the God who loves us, in heaven. We share in this new life in many ways but most deeply in the Mass, which Jesus left to his followers with the command: 'Do this in memory of me.' From that time the Mass has been at the heart of the Christian religion; it has had different names and been celebrated in many different ways but always the Church has seen it as the most important thing that we can do, since in its celebration we share in God's life by eating and drinking the bread and wine which have become the Body and Blood of Jesus.

Carlo Carretto is a member of a religious order called the Little Brothers of Jesus. Part of the preparation to become Little Brothers is to spend a week alone in a cave in the desert with only the Blessed Sacrament for company. Here is how he describes some of his experiences:*

A priest celebrates Mass; then goes away, leaving in the cave, on an altar of stones, the Eucharist [the Blessed Sacrament]. Thus, for a week one remains alone with the Eucharist exposed day and night. Silence in the desert, silence in the cave, silence in the Eucharist. No prayer is so difficult as the adoration of the Eucharist. One's whole natural strength rebels against it. . . .

To place oneself before what seems to be bread and to say, 'Christ is there, living and true,' is pure faith. . . .

Night came and I could not sleep. I left the cave, and walked under the stars above the vast desert.

'My God, I love you. My God I love you,' I shouted to the heavens through the strange silence of the night.

Without Jesus, we could not know God as a Father who loves us. We might worship God as Creator with a sort of fear, but we could not worship him with love as our Father. Jesus came to show God to us as someone who is so mighty, yet who loves us as his children.

But, some will argue, what about evil in our world. Can we worship a God who allows children to die of disease, famine or earthquake. The late William Barclay, a minister of the Church of Scotland, felt very strongly about this. He had to visit a mother whose daughter had been killed in an accident which was so impossible of explanation that the Chief Investigator could only say that it was an 'act of God.' Barclay writes:

It is difficult to imagine a more terrible and a more blasphemous phrase. What kind of God can people believe in, when they attribute the accidental death of a girl of twenty-four to an act of God. How can anyone who is left possibly pray to a God like that?

During my own parish ministry, I was never able to go into a

*Carlo Carretto, *Letters from the Desert*, Darton, Longman & Todd, 1972.

house where there had been an untimely and tragic death or sorrow and say, 'It is the will of God.' When a child or young person dies too soon, when there is a fatal accident, maybe due to someone's mistake or misjudgment, that is not an act of God, neither is it the will of God. It is, in fact, the precise opposite. It is against the will of God, and God is just as grieved about it as we are.*

God has given us the world and he wishes us to be happy. At the same time, he has given us free will and the power to choose between good and evil. Too often, we choose the evil, selfish way and close our eyes to the suffering of others. God still loves us and them, and he still cares for us and for them.

When we come to Mass on Sundays to worship God, our worship is not just to be mere words but must result in action. If we love God then we must share that love with others by living as Christians and working for a world where all the good things which God has given us will be shared with all God's children.

It's not an easy way out to be a Christian. If all people are my brothers and sisters, then I must be concerned for their welfare:

Grant me, Lord, to spread true love in the world. Grant that by me and your children it may penetrate a little into all circles, all societies, all economic and political systems, all laws, all contracts, all rulings;

Grant that it may penetrate into offices, factories, apartment buildings, cinemas, dance-halls;

Grant that it may penetrate the hearts of men and that I may never forget that the battle for a better world is a battle of love, in the service of love.

Help me to love, Lord,

not to waste my powers of love,

to love myself less and less in order to love others more and more,

That around me, no one should suffer or die because I have stolen the love they needed to live.†

*William Barclay (edited by Rita Snowden), *Into the hands of God*, Collins, 1966.
†Michel Quoist, *Prayers of Life*, Gill & Sons, 1963.

Jesus once said that the worship he wanted us to give, was 'worship in spirit and in truth' and we shall only be able to achieve this when we stop being selfish and uncaring, and realise our responsibility for God's world and its inhabitants.

You may think that we have come a long way from the common idea of worship which confines it to church on a Sunday morning, but our worship of God, our love of God, is not something only for Sunday morning, but for every day of the week, for every moment of our lives. We worship God by our prayers, by our going to Mass, and by the service we give to those who need us. We do this as followers of Jesus who came into this world so that we could come to know and love God with all our hearts.

> God hidden from our eyes,
> Men have always been searching for you.
> We probe the distance of space;
> We plumb the depths of our own minds.
> We find you, but never completely.
> Left to ourselves, we could go on searching for ever.
> Only you can bring our search to its goal.
> But you have done that:
> You have revealed yourself to us in Jesus Christ.
> As a baby he was born in a stable in Bethlehem;
> As a man he died on a cross at Calvary.
> In him our search has reached its goal.
> God hidden from our eyes.
> God hidden from our eyes,
> Yet revealed in Jesus Christ,
> We worship and adore you.*

*Caryl Micklem, *More Contemporary Prayers*, SCM Press, 1970.

CHAPTER 2

Why go to church?

On any Sunday in our towns, cities and villages, Sunday morning is fairly quiet. Usually, the only shops open are the newsagents retailing their Sunday dose of true-life confessions and passion for the majority of the population who are either in bed, or getting ready to clean the car.

However, there are signs of activity outside the various churches and chapels as people arrive to take part in their Sunday morning service. The local Catholic church, with perhaps services every hour on the hour, may be the busiest, and its unfortunate neighbours will have their slumbers disturbed by the slamming of car doors as the congregation comes together.

Why go to church?

Why go to church? Can't you pray to God just as well at home? Jesus himself said:

And when you pray, do not imitate the hypocrites: they love to say their prayers standing up in the synagogue and at the street corners for people to see them. I tell you solemnly, they have had their reward. But when you pray, go to your private room, and when you have shut your door, pray to your Father who is in that secret place, and your Father who sees all that is done in secret will reward you (Gospel of Matthew, chapter 6).

Yet, from the beginning, Christians did go to church. In the Acts of the Apostles, we read how the local Christian community in Jerusalem 'went as a body to the Temple every day but met in their houses for the breaking of the bread'.

It is true that you don't have to go to church to pray. 'Private prayer' is very important and should be part of our lives. Yet when we do go to church, we become part of a gathering of God's people in our city, town or village. Jesus said, *'where two or three meet in my name, I shall be there with them'* (Gospel of Matthew, chapter 18). So, down through the ages, Christians have come together to celebrate the Mass, to meet each other with the Lord, and to receive strength to live out their lives as Christians during the rest of the week.

The word 'church' often suggests a dark, cold, sparsely populated place whose services have little to do with life today. What we need to remember is that 'church' means people. The Church is you and I. It's not just the pope and the bishops and the priests and the nuns; it's all the people who follow Jesus and want to try to live in the way he taught us.

When we come to church, we are saying something about ourselves. We are saying that we are followers of Jesus, ready to live as Christians even if it means that we have to face up to criticism and ridicule in our world which seems to have little time for religion of any sort.

In the year 150, Justin (who later was put to death because he was a Christian) wrote down an account of the way Mass was celebrated:

On that day which is called after the sun [Sunday], all who are in the town and in the country gather together for a communal celebration. Then the memoirs of the Apostles or the writings of the Prophets are read for as long as time allows. When the reader has finished, the President speaks, exhorting us to live by these noble teachings. Then we rise all together and pray. Then, as we said earlier, when the prayer is finished, bread, wine and water are brought. The President then prays and gives thanks as well as he can. And all the people reply with the acclamation: Amen!

After this, the eucharists are distributed [communion is given] to everyone, and the deacons are sent to take them to those who are absent. Those who are well-to-do and desire to, make gifts each just as he wishes. These gifts are collected and handed over to the President. He it is who assists the orphans and the widows, those who are in want through sickness or for some other reason, prisoners, strangers passing through; briefly, who helps all who are in need.

In this description, we can recognise the Mass as we have it today. The President is the priest, who 'presides' over the celebration of the Mass. The 'memoirs of the apostles' would be the Gospels and perhaps other letters from the apostles; the writings of the prophets are from what we now call the Old Testament in the bible.

Justin gives us a picture of an open, caring, loving community which is genuinely concerned with helping 'all who are in need'. Perhaps that is what is wrong with our parishes today. We don't seem to care. We seem to be closed in on ourselves and lack concern for those who are suffering and dying at home and abroad. If our parishes were genuine loving communities, then the world would be transformed. People wouldn't be asking us why we go to church on Sundays, they would be rushing to join us!

Our Church exists today only because, at the time of Justin, Christians were so open and loving that they attracted many new followers for Christ. If there are to be Christian communities a century from now, we must regain some of the spirit which gave life to those early Christian communities. It was in the gathering together of the people to celebrate the Mass that the community was formed. It was in listening to God's word and in 'breaking the bread' (an early name for the Mass) that these Christians grew together in love, and gained the courage to bear witness to their faith in Jesus even at the cost of their own lives, dying cruel deaths in the Roman Arenas.

It is, or should be, in our assemblies each Sunday that we grow in Christ's love so that we too can be ready to bear witness to Jesus.

Why Sunday?

But why do we come together on a Sunday? Saint Justin tells us:

We hold this meeting on Sun-day because it is the first day, the day when God transformed matter and darkness and created the world, and also because it was on this same day that Jesus

Christ, our Saviour, rose from the dead. He was crucified on the eve of Saturn's day [i.e. Friday], and on the morrow of this day, that is Sun-day, he appeared to the apostles and taught them this doctrine. . . .

Another name for Sunday is the Lord's Day, because it was the day when the Lord Jesus rose from the dead. From the very earliest times, Christians have gathered on the Lord's Day to celebrate the Mass just as Jesus had commanded them. It is notable that the first meeting of Jesus with his apostles after the resurrection took place in the evening of that first Easter Sunday, and that they shared a meal. The following Sunday, he again appeared to the apostles and this time showed the wounds in his body, which he had suffered during the crucifixion, to Thomas who declared his faith, 'My Lord and my God'.

The Acts of the Apostles is a history of the early Christian Church; it gives us this description of a Sunday assembly:

On the first day of the week we met to break bread. Paul was due to leave the next day and he preached a sermon that went on till the middle of the night (Acts of the Apostles, chapter 20).

Sunday is the day we celebrate the resurrection of Jesus from the dead, and Sundays are sometimes known as 'little Easters'.

Sunday after Sunday from the time of Jesus, Christians have come together to celebrate the resurrection of the Lord by celebrating the Mass, always faithful to the Lord's command, 'Do this in memory of me.' I would like to end this chapter with this beautiful passage from *The Shape of the Liturgy* by Dom Gregory Dix:

'Do this in memory of me' – was ever another command so obeyed? For century after century, spreading slowly to every continent and country and among every race on earth, this action has been done in every conceivable human circumstance for every conceivable human need, from infancy and before it, to extreme old age and after it, from the pinnacles of earthly greatness to the refuge of fugitives in the caves and dens of the earth. Men have found no better thing than this to do for kings at their crowning and for criminals going to the scaffold; for armies in triumph or for a bride and bridegroom in a country church; for the proclamation of a dogma or for a good crop of wheat; for the wisdom of the parliament of a mighty nation or for a sick old woman afraid to die; for a schoolboy sitting an examination or for Columbus setting out to discover America; for the famine of a whole province or for the soul of a dead lover; in thankfulness that a friend did not die of pneumonia; for the repentance of a sinner or for the settlement of a strike; while the lions roared at the nearby amphitheatre; on the beach at Dunkirk; while the hiss of the scythes in the thick June grass came faintly through the windows of the church; tremulously by an old monk on the fiftieth anniversary of his vows; furtively by an exiled bishop who had hewn timber all day in a prison camp – splendidly for a canonisation – one could fill many pages with reasons why men have done this, and not tell a hundredth part of them. And best of all, week by week, and month by month, on a hundred thousand successive Sundays, faithfully, unfailingly, across all the parishes of Christendom, priest and people continue to gather in order to carry out his command, 'Do this in memory of me.'*

*Gregory Dix, *The Shape of the Liturgy*, Oxford University Press, 1945.

CHAPTER 3

What's in a church?

Growing up in our country, we are used to seeing churches – sometimes they are dull, grimy, red-brick buildings in the heart of our cities; or little village churches whose beautiful spires we glimpse across the meadows; or a great cathedral dominating a city. They may be very modern and beautiful, or modern and ugly. Everywhere we go, we come across churches and we are so used to them that we hardly notice them. Yet they are signs of a community of people, Christians, who come together each week to worship God in this special place.

It has not always been so. The first Christians met in their houses and later, when they were being persecuted, they had to meet in secret. Not for them the luxury of our churches. It wasn't until the early years of the fourth century, when the Roman Emperor Constantine allowed Christians freedom of worship, that they were able to have public buildings of their own in which to celebrate Mass. From that time, each age has built churches in different styles, but all to the honour and glory of God. You may know some of these styles, such as Gothic or Romanesque or Baroque, since many of these churches are still in use today.

Now, let's imagine that you have never been inside a Catholic church before and make your way in through the main doors, past racks selling Catholic pamphlets and books and newspapers, into the church itself.

The first thing you see is row upon row of seats or benches leading towards a large open space, called the sanctuary. If it's a modern church, the seats will be arranged in a circle or semi-circle so that everyone is as close to the sanctuary as possible. In the centre of the sanctuary is the altar, now usually in the shape of a table.

Here is the centre of the church because here the Mass is celebrated and here the body and blood of Jesus become really present. Some altars are very simple, others are more elaborate, but whatever their shape and size, they are the single most important part of any church.

Near the altar is a lectern (sometimes called an ambo); from here the scriptures are read. The lectern has an importance all its own because from here God speaks to his people in the words of scripture.

The priest's chair is in the sanctuary too. Here the priest sits during the first part of the Mass, leading the people in prayer and listening to the readings – from here he presides at Mass.

In some churches you will find that the tabernacle, in which the Blessed Sacrament is kept, is also in the sanctuary. The tabernacle is shaped something like a tiny tent, because that is what the word 'tabernacle' means. It is a reminder of how God came to live with his chosen people, the Jews, when they were a nomadic tribe and wandered from place to place, living in tents. God lives with us in the tabernacle under the form of bread. In some churches the tabernacle is not in the sanctuary but in a special Blessed Sacrament chapel. This is more in keeping with the main reasons for reserving the Blessed Sacrament in our churches: so that communion may be taken to the sick, and for private prayer and adoration. It helps to avoid confusion in the sanctuary where the real focus of attention should be the altar.

A large crucifix is in the sanctuary, too, to remind us that the Mass unites us closely with Jesus who died on the cross.

There are places for altar servers, readers and special ministers of communion to sit, and a small side table called a 'credence table' used to hold the various things which the priest will need when he celebrates Mass.

The altar itself is covered with a large white linen cloth, and there may be two or six candles on it. Candles are used as a sign of celebration, rather like at a special dinner party.

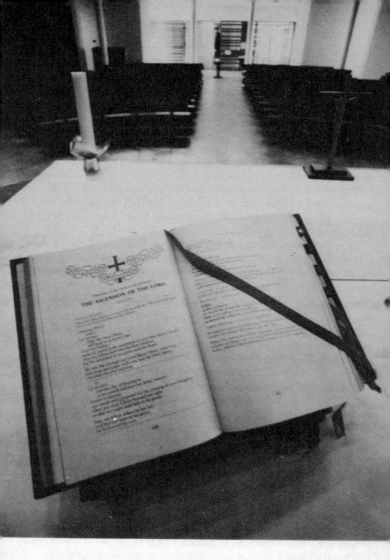

The altar is the centre of the church building, because here the Mass is celebrated

Quite often, the altar itself is bare of candles and the candles which are carried in at the beginning of Mass are placed on or near it. This ancient custom goes back to the fourth century when the carrying of candles in front of the emperor as a mark of honour was transferred to the Mass, and candles came to be carried in front of the local bishop and eventually of any celebrating priest. That is why, when the priest carries the book containing the Gospel readings to the lectern in preparation for the Gospel, candles are carried, as they are, too, in processions of the Blessed Sacrament.

The next most important part of the church is the font where baptisms take place. This is sometimes near the entrance of the church as a reminder that baptism is our entry to the Christian life. Nowadays, baptism is often celebrated during Mass. It is important that all should be able to see clearly what is happening and so the font is placed in or near the sanctuary.

Near the font will be a large candle called the paschal, or Easter, candle. This was solemnly blessed at the Easter Vigil on Holy Saturday night; it is a symbol of Jesus, the Light of the World. It is decorated with a cross; five grains of incense: to remind us of the five wounds which Jesus received before he died; A and Ω, the first and last letters of the Greek alphabet: to remind us that Jesus is the beginning and end of everything. The date of the current year is there to remind us that every year is a Year of the Lord (the letters AD, Anno Domini, mean 'in the year of the Lord'.) The paschal candle is a reminder of Jesus' rising from the dead; it often stands by the coffin at funerals to show that the one who has died has been saved by the rising of Jesus from the dead.

Another important part of the church is the confessional. Here we receive the sacrament of reconciliation in which we make our peace with God and his Church: we say that we are sorry for failing to be true followers of Jesus and God, who never ceases to love us, forgives us. Confessionals have in the past been rather gloomy, dark little rooms where we could confess our sins in complete anonymity; but since a new way of celebrating the sacrament came into use, there has been a much greater emphasis on 'face to face' confession in which we can talk to the priest about the way we are living our Christian life, instead of just reeling off a list of sins. By looking at the way we are living our lives, we come to see what is causing us to sin and can take steps to change the way we are living. Confessionals or 'Reconciliation Rooms' are becoming bright and cheerful places where people may choose to confess face to face or without being seen and recognised.

In most churches, there is an organ of some sort. This can range from a mammoth musical instrument to a humble harmonium. The organ is the traditional instrument used in church music, although many other instruments are now being used in our worship. Its presence in the church reminds us that we should lift up our voices to sing God's praises. Some churches still have a loft where the choir sings, usually quite separate from the rest of the church. However, the main job of the choir now is to lead the people in singing and it is much better if a place can be found for the choir in the main body of the church.

These, then, are the main parts of the church. Of course, you will find in any Catholic church statues of the saints to remind you that you are not alone and that these men and women have been capable, by God's grace, of living out to the full their lives as Christians. They are there as aids to prayer. Some churches have beautiful stained glass windows which are very powerful visual aids, illustrating facets of our faith. Round the walls of the church are the fourteen Stations of the Cross, used especially during Lent as visual aids to help us to follow our Lord in various incidents on his way from being condemned to death to his crucifixion and burial. Some churches have added a fifteenth Station, the Rising from the Dead.

Last but not least, you will find near the door a place from which you can take holy water to bless yourself as you enter and leave the church. When we are baptised by the pouring of water, we become Christians, followers of Jesus. As his followers we come together each week to join in the celebration of Mass and this holy water is a reminder of our baptism.

When you come to church on Sundays, the benches or seats will be filled with people. The church building has come to life. The candles are lit; there are flowers in the sanctuary. On the credence table is the chalice, which will soon contain the wine and water, covered by a veil. At the back of the church, on another table, stands a ciborium containing the hosts, or they may be on a flat dish called a paten. The ciborium looks rather like a chalice, but with a lid. Also on the table will be the wine and water. All of these will be brought up to the altar during the Offertory Procession.

When the priest enters, he will be wearing special vestments – an alb, which is the long, white vestment; the chasuble, which is the shorter vestment he wears on top of it; and the stole, which is worn round the neck, like a scarf. At one time, the priest didn't wear special vestments at all; just the ordinary clothes worn in Roman times. The alb was an indoor tunic, and the chasuble was a cloak. The stole was a sort of scarf worn by Roman officials as a sign of their rank. As time passed these ordinary clothes developed into the beautiful vestments we have today reminding us of the long history of the Mass and of how it unites generation after generation. Special vestments are not essential, of course, and in times of war and persecution they are dispensed with, but their use in our churches shows that we are taking part in a very special event.

The colour of the alb and the stole varies according to the time of the year. In Lent which is the preparation for Easter, and Advent, the preparation for Christmas, the colour is purple – it has come to be associated with the idea of penance and sorrow as we prepare for the coming of a great feast. It is also used in Masses for the Dead, when black may also be used. White, the colour of rejoicing, is used on the great feasts of our Lord such as Christmas and

Easter; on feasts of our Lady; and on feasts of saints who were not martyrs. It is becoming increasingly used in funeral Masses, to stress the fact that Christians are certain of the resurrection of the dead, and that death is not the end of everything. Red is used on feasts of our Lord's Passion – Palm Sunday and Good Friday; on feasts of the Holy Spirit; and on feasts of saints who were martyrs and gave witness to their faith by the spilling of their blood. Green is used on the Sundays and weekdays of the year which fall outside the great seasons of Easter, Lent, Christmas and Advent.

At some Masses, the priest will enter in a procession which is led by a server carrying a crucifix, with two other servers carrying candles, who are called Acolytes. Another server will carry incense. These are all signs of honour. Other servers will follow and at the end of the procession will be the special ministers of communion, the readers and the priest himself. The cross is carried at the beginning of the procession as a sign that Jesus is coming among his people to join with them in the celebration of Mass.

The church has processions at special times of the year. On Palm Sunday, there is a procession into the church to remind us of Jesus' entry into Jerusalem on the Sunday before he was to die. At the Easter Vigil on Holy Saturday night, the Easter Candle is blessed outside the church and carried into the darkness of the church as a sign that Jesus is the light of the world, bringing his light to our darkness. There are other occasions and sometimes we have special processions of the Blessed Sacrament, or in honour of our Lady.

In these and other ways, the Church helps us to take our full part in her worship. As human beings, we need signs, symbols, music, processions and colours to help us to pray, for above all else the church building is a house of prayer in which we should be able to feel at home in our prayer to the Father who loves us.

CHAPTER 4

Celebrating Jesus throughout the year

If you look in your Missal or at your Missalette next Sunday, you will see that it is, perhaps, the Twentieth Sunday in Ordinary Time, or the First Sunday of Advent, or some other number and season. Why do Sundays have numbers? Surely a Sunday is a Sunday is a Sunday. Of course, you are quite right; in the early days of Christianity the Church didn't have seasons like Advent, Lent and Easter, because the only feast kept was Sunday, the day of resurrection when everyone gathered to celebrate the Lord's day, the day on which Jesus had risen from the dead.

Celebrating Easter

The first Christians were Jews. They would have gone to the Synagogue on the Saturday evening, since Saturday, the Sabbath, is the Jewish holyday: the day on which God rested from his work of creation and on which his people too rested from all manual labour. Christians saw the Sunday as the beginning of a new creation, since Jesus had, on that day, conquered the power of death and sin. For many years Christians met together on the Saturday evening, keeping vigil until the sun rose on the Sunday when they would celebrate the 'breaking of the bread' as they remembered our Lord's command at the Last Supper, *'Do this in memory of me'*. There are several references in the New Testament which show that, even in those very early days, Sunday was the regular day for Christians to meet together.

Easter Sunday, the actual day of the Lord's resurrection, was celebrated in a special way almost from the beginning and the fifty days following it – from Easter Sunday until the feast of Pentecost when the coming of the Holy Spirit was celebrated – came to be looked on as one great celebration. The Easter Vigil was a very special Vigil and, during the course of that night, the Church celebrated the Last Supper, Christ's death on the cross, and his rising from the dead. At this time the Church did not celebrate Good Friday or Holy Thursday.

Other feasts

With the growth of Christianity and its establishment as the official religion of the Holy Roman Empire in the fourth century, pilgrims from various parts of Europe and Asia were able to go to the Holy Land to visit the places where Jesus had walked and talked and suffered and died. One of these was a nun called Egeria who went everywhere and wrote everything down in great detail for her Sisters at home. She, and others like her, brought back to the rest of the Church descriptions of the way the Church in Jerusalem celebrated the liturgy.

From these descriptions, we begin to see the beginnings of Holy Week as we now know it, with processions on Palm Sunday, the Solemn Liturgy of Christ's passion and death on Good Friday and, eventually, the celebration of the Last Supper on Holy Thursday evening. Here is Egeria's description of the Palm Sunday liturgy:

At five o'clock the passage is read from the Gospel about the children who met the Lord with palm branches, saying, 'Blessed is he that cometh in the name of the Lord.'

At this, the bishop and all the people rise from their places, and start off on foot down from the summit of the Mount of Olives. All the people go before him with psalms and antiphons, all the time repeating, 'Blessed is he that cometh in the name of the Lord.' The babies and the ones too young to walk are carried on their parent's shoulders. Everyone is carrying branches, either palm or olive, and they accompany the bishop in the very way the people did when once they went down with the Lord. They go on foot all

down the Mount to the city, and all through the city to the
Anastasis (a building round the site of the tomb of Jesus); but they
have to go pretty gently on account of the older men and women
among them who might get tired. So it is already late when they
reach the Anastasis; but even though it is late they hold the
Lucernare (a service in the evening, which involved the lighting
and blessing of lamps) when they get there. . . .*

Egeria wrote this during the fourth century; it was during
this century, too, that the Church began to keep other
special feasts such as Christmas, the birth of Jesus. The
date chosen to keep this feast was 25 December, the feast in
pagan Rome of Mithras, the sun-god of the Persians.
Gradually other feasts and seasons were added during the
year and now the Roman Calendar sets out the dates of all
the feasts in what is known as the Church's year. We may
have many feasts and seasons today, but the centre of that
year is always Easter and the centre of each week is
Sunday, the weekly celebration of Easter.

The Church's year

The Church's year begins with the *season of Advent* which
just means 'coming'. During this period of four weeks, the
Church looks forward to celebrating the coming of God as
man at Christmas; and to his coming to judge the world at
the end of time.

    Christmas is the first big feast of the year and is closely
followed by the feast of the Holy·Family. 1 January, the
beginning of the civil year is dedicated to Mary, Mother of
God, and on 6 January there is the feast of the Epiphany, a
Greek word, meaning 'showing forth'. It celebrates the
day when Jesus was shown forth to the pagans, represented by the Wise Men. The Christmas season ends with
the feast of the Baptism of the Lord, the event which
marked the beginning of Jesus' mission.

    Forty days (excluding Sunday) before Easter, the *season*

*John Wilkinson, *Egeria's Travels*, SPCK, 1971.

of Lent begins with Ash Wednesday, when blessed ashes are put on the heads of all present to remind them that Lent is a time of penance in preparation for the great feast, Easter. Penitents used to have to wear sack-cloth and ashes as a public sign of their sorrow, but now the giving of ashes is all that remains. Lent is especially a time to prepare for baptism which in the early Church was always given during the Easter Vigil.

Palm Sunday is the first day of *Holy Week*, the most sacred week of the Church's year when, like Egeria, we go in procession to recall the joyful entry of Jesus into Jerusalem. On Holy Thursday morning in the cathedral of each diocese, the Holy Oils (Chrism, used in baptism, confirmation, and ordination; Oil of the Sick; and Oil of Catechumens, used in baptism) are blessed: these will be distributed to every parish of the diocese to be used in the giving of the sacraments during the course of the year. During the evening of Holy Thursday, every parish celebrates the Mass of the Lord's Supper which reminds us of that evening when Jesus first gave himself under the forms of bread and wine to the apostles. During this Mass, we have the very beautiful ceremony of the Washing of the Feet, again in rembrance of our Lord's actions on that first Holy Thursday, and a vivid reminder that love and service are at the centre of the Christian life. On Good Friday, Mass is not celebrated. Instead we have a very simple but solemn service which includes the reading of the Passion of our Lord, and the veneration or honouring of the cross on which Jesus died for us. The service concludes with the giving of holy communion. On Holy Saturday, there are no services in the church: it is a day of mourning for Jesus lying dead in the tomb.

After sunset, the Easter Vigil begins and this really is the most important part of the whole of the Church's Year. The ceremonies include the lighting of the new fire, a sign of the new life which Jesus gives us. From this fire, the Easter Candle is lit and is seen as representing Jesus, the light of the world. The candle is carried into the darkened church

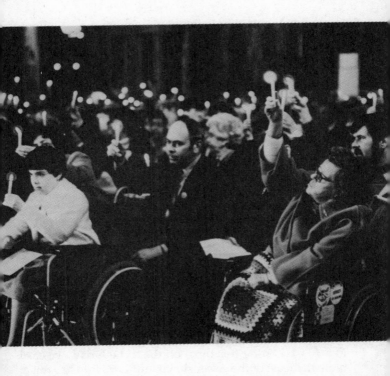

At the Easter Vigil candles are lit as a symbol of Christ's light conquering the darkness of sin, and of our sharing in the mission of bringing this light to our world

and from it the candles of all present are lit as a symbol of
Christ's light conquering the darkness of sin and of our
sharing in the mission of bringing Christ's light to our
world. A vigil consisting of several readings from the Old
Testament follows. These readings show us how God has
cared for his world and for his people from the time of the
creation, and they are completed by the readings from
the New Testament which show how Jesus conquered the
power of death by being raised from the dead on this holy
night. This is summed up in one of the prayers:

> Father,
> you teach us in both the Old and the New Testament
> to celebrate this passover mystery.
> Help us to understand your great love for us.
> May the goodness you now show us
> confirm our hope in your future mercy.

The readings from the Old and the New Testaments are
followed by the blessing of the water to be used in baptisms during the Vigil, if any are to be baptised. This water
will also be used for other baptisms during the Easter
Season.

The *Easter Season* lasts for fifty days until the feast of
Pentecost. During this time, on the fortieth day, we celebrate the feast of the Ascension of our Lord into heaven at
the end of his life on earth. Pentecost is the feast of the
coming of the Holy Spirit, and brings the Easter Season to
an end. The whole of Easter should be kept as one great
joyful feast.

The time between the season of Christmas and the
season of Lent, and the season of Easter and the season of
Advent is known as *Ordinary Time* and consists of 33 or 34
Sundays. These are the 'green' Sundays when the priest
wears green vestments. During this time we celebrate
Christ at work in our world, as the readings unfold to us
different aspects of our Lord's life and teachings.

In addition to these days, there are special feast days
commemorating various events in our Lord's life, such as

his presentation in the temple, his baptism, his trans-figuration. There are many feast days devoted to Mary and to the various saints of the Church. Throughout the course of a year, the Church celebrates not only the events of our Lord's life but also the working out of his mission in the lives of his followers.

The feasts we celebrate are not just anniversaries – not like Remembrance Day when we remember a past that has gone. In some way our celebrations make present the event that we are celebrating. For instance, when we are present at the Mass of the Lord's Supper on Holy Thursday, it is as if we were present at that supper in the Upper Room of the house in Jerusalem all those centuries ago. The Church emphasises this: on this one night the words before the consecration of the bread are altered to read:

> The day before he suffered
> to save us and all men,
> *that is today*,
> he took bread in his sacred hands

As we live through the year from Advent to Christmas, from Lent to Easter and on to Advent again, we are somehow caught up into the life of our Lord, living with him the events of his life which were the means of saving us.

CHAPTER 5

God's people come together

Inside the church, the candles are lit; the altar servers bustle about doing the thousand and one things which altar servers do. The ushers will be on duty at the door, welcoming the parishioners as they arrive, hopefully with a cheerful 'Good morning'. The usher's role is gradually becoming more important because he or she is seen as the human face of the local parish. It is the usher's job to make people feel welcome: if there are strangers, to give them hymn books and the like so that they can take their part in the Mass; and just to be a welcoming figure so that all may feel at home and be part of the community. The people chat with each other as they come in, greet their friends, and take their places.

Even today the congregation is likely to scatter itself around the church in isolated pockets. Perhaps an usher will help people to sit closer together.

Jesus promised that when two or three people meet in his name, he would be there with them. In this gathering of the people, Jesus is really present. Sometimes we have grown up with the idea that the only way Jesus is present is in the Blessed Sacrament. Of course, he is present there in a very special way, even when Mass is ended and the Sacrament is reserved in the tabernacle. But Jesus is present in other ways too, and the first of these is when his people gather in his name.

A bell rings and the procession of priest, reader and servers enters. All stand as a sign of respect as the procession makes its way round the church, led by the cross carried between two candles. In the procession, the Book of Readings or Lectionary, is carried high and with dignity, because it is the book of God's word, the book from which God speaks to his people and Christ 'proclaims his Gospel'. The priest himself comes last: he will preside over the celebration of Mass. He is another sign of Jesus' presence because when the priest celebrates the Mass, Jesus will be working through him to change the bread and wine into his body and blood.

To welcome the procession, all begin to sing a hymn or some other song. This hymn will have been carefully chosen to suit the theme of the Mass which is found in the readings: it is rather like the overture to a musical or an opera in that it sets the mood for what is to follow. It also helps the people to prepare to celebrate the Mass. A well-chosen hymn helps them turn towards God and feel at one with one another.

The priest comes to the altar, goes up to it and kisses it, because it is the most sacred part of the church, the place where the sacrifice of the Mass is offered, and Christ's body and blood are given to his people. The priest may incense the altar as a further sign of respect. He then goes to his chair where he will preside over the first part of the Mass.

His first words are a reminder that we have been called together in God's name: 'In the name of the Father, and of the Son, and of the Holy Spirit.' Everyone replies, 'Amen' which means 'so be it'. The priest then greets the people, praying that the Lord will be with them all. The late Father Clifford Howell expressed this well:

The priest speaks to you in this greeting because he recognises in you 'the assembly of chosen people belonging to the Lord', none other than the Lord himself. You are Christ's body, as St Paul says. The priest acknowledges your dignity as baptised men and women incorporated into Christ, sharing Christ's priesthood . . .*

The people reply: 'And also with you', praying that the Lord will be with the priest not only during the celebration of this Mass but in all his work as a priest of God. Here is Father Howell again:

*Clifford Howell, SJ, *Mean what you say*, Geoffrey Chapman 1965.

Make it a prayer: may the Lord be with your Spirit; may the Holy Spirit conferred on you in ordination, be ever active in you as you minister to our spiritual needs; may you always be a spiritual man, but especially now when you are taking Christ's place, saying the words and doing the actions which Christ did at the Last Supper.

The priest may now say a few words just to remind us of what we are about to do and perhaps to introduce the theme of the readings which are to follow. These few words are really intended to be the final act in welding us together as a community ready to celebrate the Mass. In a moment we shall be invited to ask the Lord's forgiveness for failing to live up to our great vocation to be his followers.

CHAPTER 6
The mercy of Jesus

Here we are, gathered in the name of Jesus, and the first thing the priest says to us after introducing us to the theme of the Mass, is

My brothers and sisters, to prepare ourselves to celebrate the sacred mysteries, let us call to mind our sins.

This leads us immediately to the question, what is sin? Today, we have new insights into the human condition. We know that what we do is, in large measure, dictated by the environment in which we live; by the way we have been brought up, by the example of our parents and their love for each other. Too often, we see this conditioning as an excuse: a reason for evading our responsibility. Is it possible for us to commit sin? Does God not love us so much that he would not take account of our little failings which were, in any case, caused by factors outside our control?

In the sixties, one of the hit stage-shows was 'West Side Story' which you have probably seen in the cinema or on television. If you have, you will remember it as a vibrant, exciting, dramatic and beautiful story set against the dreary background of the slums of New York's West Side. Here the two gangs, the Jets and the Sharks, representing the rival communities of Poles and Puerto Ricans, fight for territory in these mean, sleazy slums. But, far deeper than that, they are fighting for identity in an alien culture. They know that there is more to their lives than the tenement buildings which surround them. Deep within them they know that they are human beings and it is only within the gangs and their violent life-style that they are able to express the fact that they cannot be categorised as delinquents and therefore written off by the police and the social workers. Against this theme of violence and misery is set a beautiful love story (Romeo and Juliet transferred to New York) which culminates in the death of the hero, Tony. There were few dry eyes in the house as the audience watched Maria cradle the dead Tony in her arms and sing of that place – Somewhere – where there would be peace and quiet and open air; where there would be time to love and time to care. The story did not end there. Tony's death and Maria's love bore fruit in uniting the gangs. Out of evil came good.

It is not too far-fetched to be reminded of another Maria, cradling her dead son at the foot of the cross. The death of Jesus caused by the hatred of his own people seemed to his followers at the time to be the end; the end of a beautiful dream in which good would triumph over evil. Life had no meaning. All they could do was to hide from their enemies in the room where Jesus only the day before had celebrated a sacred meal, and had shown how much he loved them by washing their feet. Today on this dark, Bad Friday he lay dead in his mother's arms.

Of course, as we all now know, that wasn't the end. God's love for Jesus was so great that he raised him from the dead and we believe that he is living now in our world, giving meaning to the lives of everyone who believes in him, be they slum dwellers in one of the South American shanty towns or the citizens of our prosperous western society.

On that black, Bad Friday, however, the followers of Jesus did not know this. For them life had lost its meaning: this truly good man had been killed in the most barbaric way possible. Darkness had come down on the world: all they could do was hide. But then, they began to hear strange things. The tomb where Jesus had been buried was empty. Jesus had appeared to Mary Magdalen and to some of the other women. Suddenly, there he was standing in their midst, eating with them and talking to them as he used to do, bringing them the message of peace. Then, after forty days, he left them, ascending into heaven but promising to send them his Spirit who would live in them and transform their lives when he came ten days later at Pentecost. It was the same Spirit which we received when we were baptised and it is this Spirit, the Spirit of Jesus living within us, who gives new meaning to our lives.

No longer is it possible to plead that the circumstances of our lives dictate what we do. If we allow Jesus to be the Lord of our lives then we can rise above all the things which hold us back from being his true followers, just as the love of Maria and Tony was enough for them to rise above the mean slums of New York.

The fact that Jesus loves us all as individuals means that we can be responsible for the way we live; that we can do wrong; that we can sin.

But what is sin? Basically it is a turning away from God in our lives by doing things which we know to be wrong. It may be that we are lacking in love for our neighbours, our brothers and sisters in Christ, whether in our own family or those we meet in the street, in the office or on the factory floor. It may be that we ignore the poor in the Third World and do nothing at all to try to help them achieve the dignity and rights to which they are entitled as children of God.

Whatever our failing, God is ready to forgive us because he loves us and this is a wonderful thing. As St John says:

Dear friends, let us love one another, because love comes from God. Whoever loves is a child of God and knows God. Whoever does not love does not know God, for God is love. And God showed his love for us by sending his only Son into the world so that we might have life through him. This is what love is: it is not that we have loved God, but that he has loved us and sent his Son to be the means by which our sins are forgiven.

Dear friends, if this is how God loved us, then we should love one another (First Letter of Saint John, chapter 4, verses 7–12).

You are probably very familiar, perhaps too familiar, with the story which Jesus told about the Prodigal Son. Prodigal, of course, means wasteful or lavish; some commentators on the Bible have suggested that the story should really be called the 'Prodigal Father', because he loved his son so much that, despite all that he had done, he still forgave him. We are told when the son decided that he had suffered enough and it was time to go home and throw himself on his Father's mercy:

He was still a long way from home when his father saw him; his heart was filled with pity, and he ran, threw his arms round his son, and kissed him.

The son didn't have to say a word to his father – his father knew that he was sorry and out of his great love for him, he forgave him. It was only afterwards that the son said:

I have sinned against God and against you. I am no longer fit to be called your son.

The father ignored this in his joy at having his son home with him again; he called for the best robe for his son to wear and prepared a great feast to celebrate the return of his son. Perhaps we feel sympathy for the other son who had stayed faithfully at home and had done nothing wrong. His was jealous of all these celebrations and complained bitterly to his father who had to explain:

My son you are always here with me and everything I have is yours. But we had to celebrate and be happy, because your brother was dead, but now he is alive; he was lost, but now he has been found.

(You will find the story of the Prodigal Son in Luke's Gospel, chapter 15.)

It is a similar joy which Jesus tells us is felt by God our Father when we who are sinners turn once more to him and say we are sorry. The best way to do this is in the sacrament of reconciliation in which God forgives us our sins and we are helped by the priest to change our way of life so that we can follow Jesus more closely.

Here at the beginning of Mass, the Church gives us a

chance to turn to God and say: 'Father, I have sinned against you. I am no longer worthy to be called your son or daughter.' If we are sincere we will have our sins forgiven us, except for grave sins which we must confess in the sacrament of reconciliation.

You will know that there are various forms of the Penitential Rite at Mass. One is the familiar 'I confess . . .'. Another is very short; and immediately recalls the story of the Prodigal Son:

Priest	Lord, we have sinned against you:
People	Lord have mercy.
Priest	Lord, show us your mercy and love.
People	And grant us your salvation.

The third form can be very beautiful and consists of a series of statements about Jesus and his love and mercy. As we consider these, and realise how much Jesus loves us, we can only say: Lord have mercy. This is an example:

Lord Jesus, you raise us to new life: Lord have mercy.
Lord Jesus, you forgive us our sins: Christ have mercy.
Lord Jesus, you feed us with your body and blood: Lord have mercy.

Sometimes, the penitential rite of the Mass may be replaced by a beautiful ceremony which is intended to remind us of our baptism. In this, the priest blesses water and sprinkles us with it. One of the blessing prayers explains the meaning of this ceremony:

God our Father,
your gift of water
brings life and freshness to the earth;
it washes away our sins
and brings us eternal life.
We ask you now
to bless ✝ this water,
and to give us your protection on this day
which you have made your own.
Renew the living spring of your life within us

and protect us in spirit and body,
that we may be free from sin
and come into your presence
to receive your gift of salvation.

We have now received God's mercy and it is time for us, as a community, to praise God for all that he has done for us.

CHAPTER 7

Praise him!

Suddenly a great army of heaven's angels appeared with the angel, singing praises to God:
'Glory to God in the highest heaven,
and peace on earth to those with
whom he is pleased!' (St Luke's Gospel, chapter 2, verses 13–14).

We have asked for God's mercy and now we turn to him in praise and thanksgiving for all his goodness to us. Why should we praise God? Does he need our praise and thanksgiving? The Church has an answer for us:

Father, all-powerful and ever-living God,
we do well always and everywhere to give you thanks.
You have no need of our praise,
yet our desire to thank you is itself your gift.
Our prayer of thanksgiving adds nothing to your greatness,
but makes us grow in your grace,
through Jesus Christ our Lord.

This comes from one of the Prefaces of the Mass.

As a father, I love my children and as an expression of that love I do special things for them: buy them presents and take them on outings. These things are only signs of my love. I would go on doing them even if my children didn't thank me because I love them and I know that they love me, even if on occasion they might just forget to say thank you. Nevertheless, it is part of their upbringing to say thank you not just to me or their mother, but to anyone who is kind to them or who helps them in any way. The 'thank you' letter at Christmas and birthdays is part of our family life, because gratitude and praise are basic human emotions which lie at the heart of most human relationships. They are an outward expression of human love and when my small daughter says, 'Thank you, daddy' with her face aglow with pleasure, I can understand the truth of the saying that it is better to give than to receive.

So at this point in the Mass, the Church echoes the hymn that St Luke tells us the angels sang on that first Christmas when Jesus our Lord was born in the stable of Bethlehem. As we join in that glorious hymn, we know that God 'has no need of our praise', but by singing or saying it we are giving our own outward expression to our love for God our Father. We are acknowledging our relationship not with some creative power in the Universe, but with a creative person, God, who made all and cares for all and loves us as individuals, unique men and women with the vital spark of God's love within us. By acknowledging this dependence on God, we are in turn growing as human beings.

The Glory to God in the highest (the Gloria) begins by praising and thanking the Father:

> Lord God, heavenly King,
> almighty God and Father,
> we worship you, we give you thanks,
> we praise you for your glory.

We then pass on to praise Jesus, the only Son of the Father. He is called the Lamb of God. This may seem a rather strange name to us today when the only association we have with the word 'lamb' is the little white creature gambolling in the field, or the Sunday joint. To the Jews who lived at the time of Jesus, 'lamb' had several associations. The lamb was a symbol of innocence and of helplessness, but most of all it was rooted deep in the culture of their race since it was at the centre of the Passover Feast. When God commanded Moses to lead the Jews from the slavery of the Egyptians to the freedom of the Promised Land, all the Jews had to choose a lamb, which was to be killed and its blood put on the doors of their houses. The same night the lamb was to be roasted and eaten with bitter herbs and bread made without yeast:

As we join in the Glory be to God, we acknowledge our
relationship with a creative person, God who made all and cares
for all . . .

You are to eat it quickly for you are to be dressed for travel, with your sandals on your feet and your stick in your hand. It is the Passover Festival to honour me, the Lord (Exodus, chapter 12, verse 11).

The destroying angel who was to kill the first-born males of the Egyptians would recognise the houses of the Israelites marked with the blood of the lamb, and pass over them.

From then onwards the Jews kept this day as a special feast, celebrated every year exactly as described in the Book of Exodus. The lamb, to the Jew, was a sacrificial animal, who atoned to God for his chosen people's failings.

It was at Passover time that Jesus had the special meal with his disciples which we now know as the Last Supper. It was on the day before Passover that he died on the cross and it was on the day after Passover that he rose from the dead. The Church therefore sees Jesus as the Passover lamb, dying for us in order to take away our sins and then passing over from death to new life by rising from the dead on Easter day. We too, led by Jesus, are now able to pass over from the slavery of sin to the freedom of children of God because of Jesus' death and rising from the dead. That is why we praise him now as the Lamb of God who takes away the sin of the world.

The Gloria then, is the time of the Mass for us to praise God for all that he has done for us: for our families and friends; for our work; for our joys and for our sorrows. We praise him for the love he shows us every minute of the day, and above all we praise him for sending us his Son to take away our sins.

The poet, Gerald Manley Hopkins, once wrote:

It is not only prayer that gives God glory but work. Smiting on an anvil, sawing a beam, whitewashing a wall, driving horses, sweeping, scouring, everything gives God some glory if being in his grace you do it as your duty. To go to communion worthily gives God great glory, but to take food in thankfulness and temperance gives God glory too. To lift up hands in prayer gives God glory, but a man with a dung fork, a woman with a slop pail, give him glory too. He is so great that all things give him glory if you mean they should. So then, my brethren, live.

CHAPTER 8
Praying with Jesus

Our singing of the 'Glory to God' over, the priest addresses us: *Let us pray*. We might well ask ourselves, why does the priest only now ask us to pray? Haven't we been praying since we came into church?

Up to now we have been praying to God as a community, as God's people assembled; but now the priest wants us to concentrate our attention on the particular prayer for this Sunday. So he invites us to pray. He may help us to pray silently for a while by announcing some intention which will be reflected in the prayer he is about to say on behalf of the whole community, the Opening Prayer of the Mass. An example would be:

Let us pray for the strength to do God's will.

A silence follows, to allow us to think of that intention and to try to apply it to our lives. The priest would then say the Opening Prayer:

Almighty and ever-living God,
strengthen our faith, hope and love.
May we do with loving hearts
what you ask of us
and come to share the life you promise.
We make our prayer through our Lord Jesus Christ, your Son,
who lives and reigns with you and the Holy Spirit,
one God, for ever and ever.

and we all respond:

Amen.

The Opening Prayer of the Mass (or the Collect, as it is sometimes known) always follows the same pattern. First of all, God is addressed and praised (*Almighty and ever-living God*), then there is a petition (*strengthen our faith . . . share the life you promise*), and then finally we make our petition: 'Through our Lord Jesus Christ, your Son, who lives and reigns with you and the Holy Spirit, one God, for ever and ever.' You have probably heard that last phrase so often that you hardly even notice it. But it is one of the most important parts of the prayer since we are involving the whole of the Holy Trinity in our prayer, and we are reminded of how close Jesus is to us in all that we do:

I am the way, the truth and the life, no one goes to the Father except by me . . . Whoever loves me will obey my teaching. My Father will love him and my Father and I will come to him and live with him . . . The Helper, the Holy Spirit, whom the Father will send in my name will teach you everything and make you remember all that I have told you. (These quotations are all from the fourteenth chapter of St John's Gospel.)

It has long been the tradition of the Church to make prayers to the Father through the Son – especially in the Mass where Jesus is with us in a very special way. The Holy Spirit, too, is associated very closely with our prayer:

In the same way, the Spirit also comes to help us, weak as we are. For we do not know how we ought to pray: the Spirit himself pleads for us . . . (St Paul's letter to the Romans, chapter 8, verse 26).

The Opening Prayers of the Mass are sometimes very short, but they say a great deal about our attitude to and relationship with God, reminding us first of his love for us and praising him for this love; then making our request of our loving Father. This pattern is in fact that taught to the disciples by Jesus.

One day Jesus was praying in a certain place. When he had finished, one of his disciples said to him, 'Lord, teach us to pray, just as John taught his disciples.' Jesus said to them, 'When you pray, say this:

Father,
May your holy name be honoured;
may your kingdom come.
Give us day by day the food we need.
Forgive us our sins,
    for we forgive everyone who does us wrong.
And do not bring us to hard testing.'
(St Luke's Gospel, chapter 11).

If we wish to pray with Jesus at Mass and at home, then we should try to follow the pattern of the prayer given there – and, of course, we should not limit our prayer to the Mass. The public prayer of the Mass should flow out into our private lives, so that it gives us the wish, the desire, the longing to pray in the privacy of our own homes as a family or as individuals. Similarly, the growth of our private life of prayer will help us to join even more fully in the prayer of the Mass, which is the greatest of all prayers because it is not just a human action but an action which unites the divine and the human: Jesus himself is there praying with us to his Father.

As followers of Jesus, it is up to us to call other people to pray and this can only be done if we ourselves are men and women of prayer. It is not possible to teach other people how to pray, but our example can give them the desire to pray. In the extract from St Luke, the disciples first saw Jesus praying, and this awakened in them the desire to know how to do it properly.

If we believe . . . that through every Mass Christ really unites himself to us, then we will expand and grow in his greatness. We will be given new eyes, new ears, we will be given a new heart, a new mind: and this will happen continuously in Christ.*

There is one disadvantage of the Roman prayers which we have in our Missal, and that is that they are so concise that they are finished almost before they have begun. So longer, alternative prayers have been provided for Sundays and

*E. J. Farrell, *Prayer is a hunger*, Dimension Books, N.J., 1972.

the major feasts and many of these are extremely beautiful.
Here are a few examples:

> Almighty God and Father of light,
> a child is born for us and a son is given to us.
> Your eternal Word leaped down from heaven
> in the silent watches of the night,
> and now your Church is filled with wonder
> at the nearness of her God.
> Open our hearts to receive this life
> and increase our vision with the rising of dawn,
> that our lives may be filled with his glory and peace
> who reigns for ever and ever. (Christmas: Dawn Mass)
>
> ●
>
> God our Father,
> your Word, Jesus Christ, spoke peace to a sinful world
> and brought mankind the gift of reconciliation by
> the suffering and death he endured.
>
> Teach us, the people who bear his name,
> to follow the example he gave us:
> may our faith, hope and charity
> turn hatred to love, conflict to peace,
> death to eternal life. (4th Sunday of Lent)
>
> ●
>
> Father of light, from whom every good gift comes,
> send your Spirit into our lives
> with the power of a mighty wind,
> and by the flame of your wisdom
> open the horizons of our minds.
> Loosen our tongues to sing your praise
> in words beyond the power of speech,
> for without your Spirit
> man could never raise his voice in words of peace
> or announce the truth that Jesus is Lord,
> who lives and reigns with you and the Holy Spirit,
> one God, for ever and ever. (Pentecost)

We can use these beautiful prayers as meditations in our
own prayers at home as we prepare to come to Mass to join
with the priest in prayer to God our Father.

Part Two

GOD SPEAKS...
...WE RESPOND

The Liturgy of the Word

CHAPTER 9

God speaks to us

Black Elk Speaks

My friend, I am going to tell you the story of my life, as you wish; and if it were only the story of my life I think I would not tell it; for what is one man that he should make much of his winters, even when they bend him like a heavy snow? So many other men have lived and shall live that story, to be grass upon the hills.

It is the story of all life that is holy and is good to tell, and of us two-leggeds sharing in it with the four-leggeds and the wings of the air and all green things; for these are the children of one mother and their father is one Spirit.*

Every culture has its own folk history – its own legends and stories of how it came into being. Such stories, first told round camp fires or by wandering minstrels, were passed on from generation to generation by word of mouth. They told of life and of creation from the point of view of the story-teller and his tribe.

When we look at the enormous book which is the Bible, we may find it difficult to realise that much of it came into being in the same way – stories told round a campfire by a nomadic people, wandering the deserts and gradually coming to terms with their special relationship with God.

Black Elk Speakes, Barrie & Jenkins, 1972.

The part of the Bible which we now know as the Old Testament is really a number of books written down at different times and in different places. It is made up of legends, histories, poetry, teaching, sermons and prophecies – all with their own particular style.

The story of Jesus' life and his teachings were also passed by word of mouth at first, before being collected and written down to form the four Gospels of Matthew, Mark, Luke and John. In fact the first Gospel (a word which means 'Good News') wasn't written down until over thirty years after the death of Jesus. The New Testament contains the Gospels, the Acts of the Apostles (the story of the early Church), various letters from Paul and other apostles to the Christians in various towns and cities of the Roman Empire, and a rather strange book called the Book of Revelation (or Apocalypse) in which St John describes a dramatic vision he had.

We believe that God has spoken to his people in the Old and the New Testaments, telling us about himself and his care for us. The Church continues to tell us about God in the Mass in the Liturgy of the Word. This consists of a reading from the Old Testament, a psalm, a reading from one of the letters of the New Testament, a Gospel acclamation, the Gospel itself, a homily (or sermon), the Creed, and the Prayer of the Faithful.

All that has gone before has been a preparation for this part of the Mass. As a community, we have come together, asked God's forgiveness, praised him and prayed to him. Now we are ready to listen to him speaking to us in the words of the scriptures.

Saint Paul described the word of God as something alive and active. Saint Jerome said that to be ignorant of the scriptures was to be ignorant of Christ. If we close our minds to the scriptures, we close our minds to God. Some people say that the scriptures are far too difficult to understand and there are certainly some very difficult passages. But Mark Twain had a point when he said:

Most people are bothered by those passages in Scripture which they cannot understand; but, as for me, I always noticed that the passages in Scripture which trouble me most are those that I do understand.

When we speak to someone we expect a reply. There can be nothing more hurtful than for a person to talk about his or her plans or problems only to find that the person they are speaking to has not been listening. When the word of God is read in church, God is speaking to you and he expects a reply. If you don't listen to what God is saying to you, or don't take the trouble to find out how you can put God's word into practice in your life, you are ignoring God, and his message for you that day is lost.

The Lectionary

The book containing all the readings for use at Mass is called the Lectionary. It is very large (in fact, the new edition is in three volumes) and provides readings not only for Sundays, but for weekdays, for the feasts of the saints, and for special occasions such as Christian Unity, and for the celebration of the sacraments such as baptism and marriage. You will find excerpts from it in your Sunday Missal or Weekday Missal.

So that we can hear as much of the bible as possible on Sundays, the readings have been arranged over a three year period. In that period of time, most of the New Testament is read at Sunday Mass.

The Lectionary for Sundays was put together with a view to giving the Gospel pride of place in the readings. In the first year of the three year cycle of readings – which is known as Year A – the Gospel of Matthew is read; in year B, the Gospel of Mark; and in year C, the Gospel of Luke. Matthew, Mark and Luke are known as the *synoptic* gospels, because their authors saw the events of our Lord's life 'with one eye', i.e. from the same point of view, which is what 'synoptic' means. They are in the form of a narrative or history of Jesus and were written down fairly soon after the death of Jesus. St John's Gospel, written much later, is more of a meditation on the events of our Lord's life in which John, guided by the Holy Spirit, tries to bring out the full depths of Jesus' message for the Christian people. John has always been thought of as a very special Gospel and in the lectionary it is used during the great seasons of Easter and Lent.

The Gospel readings follow on in sequence from Sunday to Sunday, so that we can follow the development of Jesus' life and teaching; each of the Gospels can speak for itself and we are able to see how each of them gives us a different portrait of Jesus but at the same time proclaims the basic message of the Gospel: Jesus is Lord.

The first reading at Mass is chosen from the Old Testament (except during the season of Easter when the Acts of the Apostles is read). For many of us, the Old Testament is something of a closed book, but for Jesus it was *the* Bible. He knew it and it formed his thought and his preaching:

He came to Nazareth, where he had been brought up, and went into the synagogue on the sabbath day as he usually did. He stood up to read, and they handed him the scroll of the prophet Isaiah. Unrolling the scroll he found the place where it is written:
'The spirit of the Lord has been given to me,
for he has anointed me.
He has sent me to bring the good news to the poor,
to proclaim liberty to captives
and to the blind new sight,
to set the downtrodden free,
to proclaim the Lord's year of favour.'
He then rolled up the scroll, gave it back to the assistant and sat down. And all eyes in the synagogue were fixed on him. Then he began to speak to them, 'This text is being fulfilled today even as you listen.' And he won the approval of all, and they were astonished by the gracious words that came from his lips (from the Gospel of Luke, chapter 4).

Here at the beginning of his mission of preaching, Jesus used the Old Testament prophecy of Isaiah as a sort of manifesto. This was to be his policy; he had been anointed by God and he was the fulfilment of all the prophecies in the Old Testament. Later, after his death and rising from the dead, he appeared to two of his followers on the way to Emmaus, a village near Jerusalem. Somehow, they didn't recognise him, but as they walked, 'starting with Moses and going through all the prophets, he explained to them the passages throughout scripture which were about himself' (from the Gospel of Luke, chapter 24).

The Old Testament reading at Mass has been chosen with the Gospel reading in mind. You will find that this reading always refers to the Gospel in some way. It may be that in the Gospel passage Jesus quotes from the Old Testament, or there may be a parallel for some action of Jesus, such as the curing of lepers, or there may be a contrast between the attitude of the Old Testament and the teaching of Jesus. In this way, we see Jesus as the fulfilment of the Old Testament, but we can also see our faith as being a continuation of the Jewish faith – a reminder that God first revealed himself to the Jews, his chosen people. In the Mass, we refer to Abraham, the founder of the Jewish people, as 'our Father in faith'.

After the first reading comes a psalm, which we say or sing, as a meditation on what we have just listened to (we say more about this in chapter 10).

The second reading is always taken from the letters of the apostles – most frequently from Paul. Except in the major seasons of Easter, Lent, Christmas and Advent, they have no connection with the theme of the Gospel reading, but are read in sequence from Sunday to Sunday. This helps us to follow the development of the letter-writer's thought from beginning to end and gives us an insight into the life of the early church. Many of the problems they faced are still faced by the Church today; as we listen to Paul, Peter, James or John we come to a clearer understanding of how we in our turn must try to bring the good news of Jesus to our own town or city or village.

Before the reading of the Gospel, we stand for an acclamation to the Gospel. Jesus, really present in his

Gospel, will be speaking to us; so we stand to welcome him with song, as the book of the Gospels is solemnly carried from the altar to the lectern, preceded by servers carrying incense and candles.

After the Gospel, we sit for the homily, or sermon, in which the priest applies the teaching of the Gospel to our lives. The Gospels and the letters of the apostles were written almost two thousand years ago, in conditions very different from our own times, yet their message is still relevant today. The purpose of the homily is to make the Gospels live for us here and now, and it is one of the most difficult things that a priest has to do. The ideal homily is one which is based firmly on the readings of the Mass, is not too long (7–10 minutes) and manages to stay on the subject! It should help us to live as Christians.

In this part of the Liturgy of the Word, God has spoken to us. We ought to be ready to receive his message and some of us may find it helpful to prepare for each Sunday by reading the scripture readings and praying about them either alone or as a family. If we do this, the scriptures will really come alive for us and we will be happy to respond to God when he speaks to us.

CHAPTER 10

The psalms – the prayers of Jesus

One of the best-known books of the Old Testament is the Book of Psalms. The Church uses it a great deal – in the Mass, and as the major part of the Liturgy of the Hours (also called the Divine Office) which is the daily prayer of priests, monks, nuns and an ever-increasing number of lay people.

The Book of Psalms was the daily prayer of the Jews and therefore of Jesus. As a good Jew, he would often have heard the psalms sung as part of the religious services, and we know from the Gospels that he was very familiar with them since he used them in his teaching.

There are 150 psalms in the bible, written at various periods of Old Testament times. Some are very beautiful, full of love and praise; some are ugly and full of hatred; some are meditations and others are great shouts of joy and praise. The psalms can match all our different moods:

No one who takes the words of the psalms on his lips and their meaning in his heart, who allows the rhythm of their images to take hold of him and their accents to echo through his being, can possibly remain indifferent to them. They may overwhelm or shock, bring peace or exaltation, but inevitably they draw us beyond ourselves; they force us to that meeting with God without whom we cannot live and who transforms our whole life.*

We can see this if we look at extracts from some of the psalms:

*J. Gelineau, SJ, *The Psalms: a new translation*, Fontana, 1966.

Psalm of Praise
Alleluia!

Praise the Lord from the heavens,
praise him in the heights.
Praise him, all his angels,
praise him, all his host.

Praise him, sun and moon,
praise him, shining stars.
Praise him, highest heavens
and the waters above the heavens. (Psalm 148)

Psalm of Trust
O Lord, you search me and you know me,
you know my resting and my rising,
you discern my purpose from afar.
You mark when I walk or lie down,
all my ways lie open to you. . . . (Psalm 138)

Psalm of Sorrow
My offences truly I know them;
my sin is always before me.
Against you, you alone, have I sinned;
what is evil in your sight I have done. (Psalm 50)

Historical Psalm
He threatened the Red Sea; it dried up
and he led them through the deep as through the desert.
He saved them from the hand of the foe;
he saved them from the grip of the enemy.

The waters covered their oppressors;
not one of them was left alive.
Then they believed in his words
then they sang his praises. (Psalm 105)

Meditation on the shortness of life
You turn men back into dust
and say: Go back, sons of men.
To your eyes a thousand years
are like yesterday, come and gone,
no more than a watch in the night. (Psalm 89)

Psalm of longing
By the rivers of Babylon
there we sat and wept
remembering Zion:
on the poplars that grew there
we hung up our harps.

For it was there that they asked us,
our captors, for songs,
our oppressors, for joy.
'Sing to us,' they said,
'one of Zion's songs.'

O how could we sing
the song of the Lord
on alien soil? (Psalm 136)

These few examples show the wonderful variety of the psalms. When they are used often as part of daily prayer, we come to love them and as we get to know them better, they become part of our way of thinking.

Hearing them every Sunday in the Mass, we become familiar with certain word pictures and certain attitudes towards God. The psalm follows on after the first reading and we know it now as the Responsorial Psalm. It is a meditation on the first reading and a response to it. We have heard God's word and we respond to it by singing this song which helps us to reflect on the message of the reading. For instance, on the Third Sunday of Year A, the first reading is from the prophet Isaiah and includes the famous passage:

The people that walked in darkness
has seen a great light;
on those who live in a land of deep shadow
a light has shone.

The Response makes quite clear who the light is:

The Lord is my light and my help.

and this is taken up by the psalm itself:

> The Lord is my light and my help;
> whom shall I fear?
> The Lord is the stronghold of my life;
> before whom shall I shrink. (Psalm 26)

It is important that we take our part in the responsorial psalm by making the response, whether it is sung or said. St John Chrysostom who lived in the fourth century explained why this participation is so important:

If you sing, 'As a deer longs for running streams, so my soul is longing for you, my God,' you make a covenant with God, you sign a pact with him, though without ink or paper. Your voice proclaims that you love him above everything, that you prefer nothing to him, that you burn with love for him.

Perhaps we can learn to sing our part of the psalm so that we too burn with love for the God who loves and cares for us.

CHAPTER 11

We speak to God

God has spoken to us – in the readings from scripture and in the homily we have heard his voice and now it is time to make our response. We do this by making together a profession of our faith and praying to God in the Prayer of the Faithful which we also call the Bidding Prayer.

Our profession of faith (or Creed) is based on a statement of belief which was compiled at Nicea in 325 AD; hence it is known as the Nicene Creed. It was the product of a Council which brought together the bishops of the Church to discuss problems facing the Church at that time. At first it was used in the service of baptism by those who were about to be received into the Church.

Nowadays, in the Mass, the Nicene Creed is used as a summary of our faith – the faith of the whole parish community; therefore the first words are: *We believe*. . . .

The Creed is in three parts. The first is a statement of our belief in God the Father who created everything:

> maker of heaven and earth
> of all that is, seen and unseen.

The second part concerns Jesus, *the only Son of God*, who became incarnate from the Virgin Mary and was made man.

We recall that he

> was crucified under Pontius Pilate;
> he suffered death and was buried.

We express our belief that

On the third day he rose again in accordance with the scriptures; he ascended into heaven
and is seated at the right hand of the Father.

These are the events on which our faith is based. We believe that Jesus still lives in heaven with his Father and we go on:

> He will come again in glory to judge the living and the dead, and his kingdom will have no end.

We look forward to the end of time when Christ will come to receive us into God's kingdom.

The third part of the Creed deals with our belief in the Holy Spirit, *the Lord, the giver of life*, and how he works through the Church. We recall that the Holy Spirit *has spoken through the Prophets* and now he speaks through the *one, holy, catholic and apostolic Church*. 'Catholic' in this sense means universal; a reminder that the Church exists throughout the world. It is 'apostolic' because it can trace its origins back to the time of the apostles and still teaches the message of the apostles. Since the creed was said immediately before baptism, it is natural that it includes a statement of belief in *one baptism for the forgiveness of sins*. As in the second part, the third ends by looking forward to the end of time:

> We look for the resurrection of the dead, and the life of the world to come. Amen.

As we have said, this Creed was first used in baptisms, and it is right that our response to God's word, to which we have been listening, should be an expression of the faith into which we were baptised. In fact, on Easter Sunday, the Creed is replaced by the promises made in the service of Baptism in a dialogue between priest and people:

Priest Do you reject Satan?
All   I do
Priest And all his works?
All   I do
Priest And all his empty promises?
All   I do

Priest	Do you believe in God, the Father almighty, creator of heaven and earth?
All	I do
Priest	Do you believe in Jesus Christ, his only Son, our Lord, who was born of the virgin Mary, was crucified, died and was buried, rose from the dead, and is now seated at the right hand of the Father?
All	I do
Priest	Do you believe in the Holy Spirit, the holy Catholic Church, the communion of saints, the forgiveness of sins, the resurrection of the body, and life everlasting?
All	I do

As baptised Christians, we are able to pray to God our Father, because in baptism we have become his sons and daughters. We now turn to our Father in the Prayer of the Faithful, the special prayer of baptised Christians. This, too, is a response to God's word since, if we are to put his word into practice in our world, we shall need the strength and grace which only God can give us.

St Paul, writing to Timothy, one of his followers, gives us an example of what our prayer should be about:

My advice is that, first of all, there should be prayers offered for everyone – petitions, intercessions and thanksgiving – and especially for kings and others in authority, so that we may be able to live religious and reverent lives in peace and quiet (from Paul's first letter to Timothy, chapter 2).

The Prayer of the Faithful follows a simple pattern. First there is a short invitation to prayer, such as:

> Let us turn in prayer to God our Father
> who loves and cares for us.

This is said by the priest and then the Reader will make various petitions which are usually arranged in this way:

1. For the Church
2. For those in authority

3. For the poor and the needy
4. For the local community

The petitions should be short and simple; they are invitations to us to pray for each intention. There should always be a moment of silence to allow us to make them our own, before we all say the response, such as 'Lord, hear our prayer'. That short response is, in fact, our prayer. In England and Wales, the petitions are followed by the prayer to our Lady, the Hail Mary. Then comes a moment of silent prayer to allow us to pray for our own needs in the light of the Gospel we have heard. The Prayer of the Faithful ends with a prayer said by the priest, asking God to accept our petitions and prayers.

Sometimes when we have Mass in a home, we can make our petitions spontaneously but we should try not to be inward-looking but always to be aware that the Prayer of the Faithful is concerned with the whole Church and the whole world.

The Liturgy of the Word has come to an end with prayer. God has spoken to us and we have made our reply: a reply of faith and trust in a God who loves each one of us and who is always ready to listen to us. As we pause in silence before the Liturgy of the Eucharist begins, we give thanks to God for the gift of his Son who has spoken to us and called us to be his followers.

Part Three

TAKE AND EAT ...
... TAKE AND DRINK
The Liturgy of the Eucharist

CHAPTER 12

'Do this as a memorial of me'

If you look at your Mass Book, you will see that there are two main parts of the Mass: the Liturgy of the Word and the Liturgy of the Eucharist. In the Liturgy of the Word, we listen to God's word in the Scriptures and respond to it by professing our faith when we say the Creed, and by praying for the needs of our world in the Prayer of the Faithful. This leads on to the second part of the Mass, the Liturgy of the Eucharist.

Eucharist is based on a Greek word which means *'thanksgiving'*; it is a name often given to the whole of the Mass, because in the Mass we really give thanks to God the Father for the life, death and resurrection of Jesus who, by the power of his Spirit, still lives in the Church. In the Mass he gives us his body to eat and his blood to drink so that we are completely united with our God and Father.

St Paul, writing to the Christians at Corinth, handed on the Church's tradition concerning that sacred night, Holy Thursday, when Jesus first changed bread into his body, and wine into his blood:

This is what I received from the Lord, and in turn passed on to you: that on the same night that he was betrayed, the Lord Jesus took some bread and thanked God for it and broke it, and he said, 'This is my body which is for you; do this as a memorial of me.' In the same way he took the cup after supper and said, 'This cup is the new covenant in my blood. Whenever you drink it, do this as a memorial of me.' Until the Lord comes, therefore, every time you eat this bread and drink this cup, you are proclaiming his death (from the first letter of St Paul to the Corinthians, chapter 11, verses 23–26).

This is probably the earliest description we have of the Last Supper, since St Paul is believed to have written this letter before the Gospels themselves were written down and it shows how, from the very beginning, the Church carried out the Lord's command – *Do this as a memorial of me.*

When we use the word 'memorial', we don't think of the Mass as being just a remembering of something which happened a long time ago. In some way, we believe that when Mass is celebrated, the events of two thousand years ago are made present and we are joined with Jesus and his apostles just as if time and space did not exist.

In the Liturgy of the Eucharist, the Church follows the actions of Jesus:

1. The priest *takes* bread and wine at the beginning of this part of the Mass (the Preparation of the Gifts).

2. The priest *thanks* God for the bread and wine in the Eucharistic Prayer and Jesus acting through the priest blesses them so that they become his body and blood.

3. The priest *breaks* the bread just before he distributes communion.

4. The priest *gives* us the bread (and sometimes the wine) and in communion we receive the body and blood of Jesus just as the apostles did from his hands at that last supper in an upper room in Jerusalem hundreds of years ago.

Do we really believe that the bread and wine can become the body and blood of Jesus? Do we really believe that God has power to suspend all the laws of nature and turn bread and wine into his body and blood?

St John describes such a trial of faith during the life of Jesus. Jesus had told the crowd:

> I am the living bread which has come down from heaven.
> Anyone who eats this bread will live for ever;
> and the bread that I shall give
> is my flesh, for the life of the world.

The crowd started to argue saying, 'How can this man give us his flesh to eat?' but Jesus was not deterred and repeated his statement even more strongly. Many of his followers then said:

'This is intolerable language. How could anyone accept it?' Many of his disciples left him and stopped going with him.

Then Jesus said to the Twelve (apostles), 'What about you, do you want to go away too?' Simon Peter answered, 'Lord, who shall we go to? You have the message of eternal life, and we believe; we know that you are the Holy One of God' (from chapter 6 of the Gospel according to St John).

It is quite obvious that this was a crucial part of the message Jesus meant to leave to his Church. It was a crisis point and he risked losing even his twelve closest friends, the apostles, so important was this teaching. He could have said, 'Of course I don't mean it literally. How could you really eat my flesh and drink my blood? Don't be silly! I am just talking in parables.' But he didn't, and some of his followers left him.

Each time we come to Mass, we are faced with the choice Jesus gave to the crowd – do we find this teaching 'intolerable' or do we accept that Jesus has the message of eternal life and the power to give us himself – his body and blood to eat and drink?

CHAPTER 13
Offering ourselves with Jesus

In Chapter 2, we read St Justin's description of the Mass as it was celebrated in his day. After the Bidding Prayer, bread, wine and water were brought to the 'president' of the assembly and, later in the Mass, a collection was taken for the poor and needy and given to the 'president' to distribute.

As time passed, the offertory procession grew and developed. Families provided bread and wine which they themselves had made to be used in the Eucharist. How powerful is this sign of the blessing of all human work, when the bread and wine produced by the families of the parish are used to become the body and blood of Jesus. In our own times, this custom is being revived, especially when Mass is celebrated in people's homes.

Gradually another custom developed: the bringing of material gifts – gold, silver, money and produce – to the altar for the use of the priest and the Church's service of the poor. Unfortunately, with the passing of time and a gradual decline in the active participation of the people in the celebration of the Mass, the offertory procession disappeared completely and we were left only with the collection of money. You will hear many jokes about the collection and it would seem that no Catholic function is really complete without it. Yet the collection is important – giving money is a symbol of our giving of ourselves, our daily lives, to the service of God in the Church.

In our present celebration of Mass, the Offertory Procession has been restored and the gifts of bread and wine, together with the collection, are brought to the altar. The bread and wine will become the Body and Blood of Jesus; the money will be used in the service of the Church. The procession is a sign of the offering of ourselves, of our lives, to God. Sometimes, especially in school Masses, examples of the children's work are carried to the altar to symbolise in as vivid a way as possible the connection between the Mass and the living out of our Christian lives.

Too often, we could be accused of being 'Sunday Christians' with our faith in a little box which we open for an hour (or less) on a Sunday morning, only to close it and put it away for the rest of the week when we leave the church at the end of Mass. The Offertory Procession is a reminder that this is not so: that our faith is a part of us, like breathing or eating, and that what we do in church on a Sunday morning finds expression in what we do on the other six days of the week.

In the Acts of the Apostles, we find this description of the Christian community shortly after the death, resurrection and ascension of Jesus:

The early Christians remained faithful to the teaching of the apostles, to the brotherhood, to the breaking of bread, and to prayers . . . The faithful all lived together and owned everything in common; they sold their goods and possessions and shared out the proceeds among themselves according to what each one needed.

They went in a body to the Temple every day but met in their houses for the breaking of bread; they shared their food gladly and generously; they praised God and were looked up to by everyone (from the Acts of the Apostles, chapter 2).

In this description, we see a community in which there were no artificial barriers between prayer and action. These Christians worked and prayed together and cared for one another. Of course, it was a long time ago and people will say that it could not work in our large industrialised cities. Yet the world today has been called a 'global village' because the various means of communication – radio, television, and so on – make us vividly aware of what is happening to our brothers and sisters in the poor nations and disturbed areas of our world. We are called as Christians to pray together and to care for one another. We

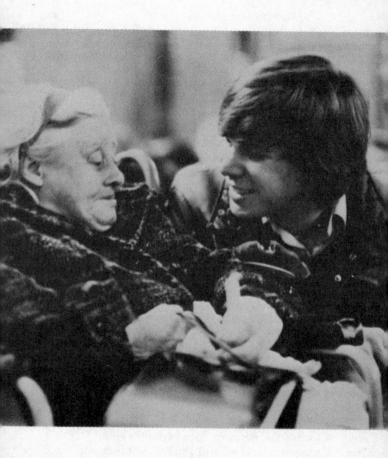

Just what are we offering? . . . are we really trying to live as
followers of Jesus?

must try to devise ways and means of making our communities more open and caring not just for the needs of our immediate neighbours, but for our neighbours throughout the world.

Every time we come to Mass, we ought to be challenged by the awareness that, while we who are rich are joining in this celebration in our comfortable church building, many of our brothers and sisters are dying in other parts of the world. The Offertory is a point in the Mass when our daily lives (represented by the money in the collecting plate) are brought before God in a special way. We must ask ourselves just what we are offering. Is it the first-fruits of our lives; are we really going to try to live as followers of Jesus?

When Jesus celebrated his Last Supper on Holy Thursday and left us the Mass to celebrate until the end of time, he chose bread and wine to become his Body and Blood because bread and wine were the basic food and drink of the community in which he lived. Even today, bread is probably still our most basic food. More important still, bread and wine show clearly how the human race co-operates with God in making food: this is beautifully expressed in the two Blessing Prayers which the priest offers over the bread and wine when they are brought to the altar:

> Blessed are you, Lord, God of all creation.
> Through your goodness we have this bread to offer,
> which earth has given and human hands have made.
> It will become for us the bread of life.

and

> Blessed are you, Lord, God of all creation.
> Through your goodness we have this wine to offer,
> fruit of the vine and work of human hands.
> It will become our spiritual drink.

These blessing prayers are based on Jewish family table prayers and are very similar to the prayers which Jesus may have said at the Last Supper. In them the priest praises God for his goodness in giving us bread 'which earth has given and human hands have made', and wine 'fruit of the vine and work of human hands'. This partnership between God and man is a wonderful thing and another reminder of the interplay of what we do at Mass and what we do in our daily lives.

Before the Blessing Prayer is said over the wine, a little water is added to the chalice (or cup). At the time of Jesus it was a Greek practice, observed in Palestine, to add water to the wine. This has been continued by the Church down the centuries and is now seen as a symbol of our unity with Jesus – just as the wine absorbs the water which then becomes inseparable from it, so does Jesus absorb us into his body. So the water is seen as a symbol of ourselves: our lives, and all our weaknesses.

At solemn Masses, the gifts of bread and wine are now incensed, to show that they are set apart for a special purpose: to be offered to God our Father when they become the Body and Blood of Jesus in the Eucharistic Prayer.

The priest washes his hands which originally had the practical purpose of cleaning them after he had been handling the various gifts brought up in the Offertory Procession. Now it has a symbolic meaning, showing that the priest is of himself unworthy to offer the great sacrifice of the Mass. He says quietly:

Lord, wash away my iniquities: cleanse me from my sins.

The priest invites us all to pray and says the Prayer over the Gifts which states clearly the meaning of all that has gone before and what will follow. The following prayer from the Mass of the 25th Sunday in Ordinary Time is a good example:

Lord God,
in this bread and wine
you give us food for body and spirit.

> May the eucharist renew our strength
> and bring us health of mind and body.
> We ask this in the name of Jesus the Lord.

The Prayer over the Gifts brings this part of the Mass to an end. The gifts have been prepared and set aside and we are ready now to begin the central part of the Mass, the Eucharistic Prayer.

CHAPTER 14

Let us give thanks

As we saw earlier, the word Eucharist means thanksgiving. The prayer at the very heart of the Mass is the Eucharistic Prayer in which we give thanks for God's great goodness to us, and join with the priest in offering sacrifice to God our Father. Once again, in the liturgy, time has no meaning and we are joined with Jesus in offering that one great sacrifice which he made when he died on the cross. It is obviously impossible for any human words to do justice to this happening: in the early days of Christianity there was no single form of Eucharistic Prayer and the celebrating priest would use his own words, expressing his faith in the great mystery. As time passed, the prayer became standardised and for several centuries the Western part of the Catholic Church had only one Eucharistic Prayer, known as the Canon of the Mass. This is now our Eucharistic Prayer I. In the Eastern Catholic Churches, there were always several forms of Eucharistic Prayer.

Today in the Roman Catholic Church, we have nine Eucharistic Prayers approved for use throughout the world. There are the four you will find in most Mass books; two for Masses of Reconciliation which can be used during Lent or in Masses for peace; and three for use in Masses with children. Although there are some differences between them, (especially in Eucharistic Prayer I), the prayers have the same basic structure.

All begin with a dialogue between priest and people:

Priest	The Lord be with you.
People	And also with you.
Priest	·Lift up your hearts.
People	We lift them up to the Lord.
Priest	Let us give thanks to the Lord.
Priest	It is right to give him thanks and praise.

In this very solemn way we are invited to raise our hearts in prayer to prepare to take our part in the Eucharistic Prayer.

All the Eucharistic Prayers begin with what is called a Preface in which we give thanks to God and remember some special way in which he has shown his love for us. This can be seen at its clearest and simplest in the Preface to one of the Eucharistic Prayers for children:

> God our Father,
> you have brought us here together
> so that we can give you thanks and praise
> for all the wonderful things you have done.
>
> We thank you for all that is beautiful in the world
> and for the happiness you have given us.
> We praise you for daylight
> and for your word which lights up our minds.
> We praise you for the earth
> and all the people who live on it
> and for our life which comes from you.
>
> We know that you are good.
> You love us and do great things for us.

Having listened to the priest thanking God on our behalf, we take part in singing his praises in the very ancient Christian hymn sometimes called by its Latin name, the Sanctus.

> Holy, holy, holy Lord, God of power and might,
> heaven and earth are full of your glory.
> Hosanna in the highest.
> Blessed is he who comes in the name of the Lord.
> Hosanna in the highest.

Suddenly we are reminded of that day outside Jerusalem when the crowd threw palm branches and their cloaks down in front of Jesus as he entered the city, riding on a donkey – the sign of a man of peace and humility. Again we hear their cheers: *Hosanna to the Son of David* and remember too how those cheers changed to jeers as they called out *Crucify him! Crucify him!* a few days later on Good

Friday. The 'Holy, holy, holy' is a reminder to us as we begin this most special part of the Mass, of how easy it is to lose the enthusiasm we feel in church, so that even we may betray our Lord in the way we live our lives.

Our worship is not just something earthly however. It is not confined by the bonds of time and space. In some way that we cannot understand, the Mass exists outside time and space, in eternity, and when we join in this celebration wherever it may be, we are united not just with those who are present here and now, but with all those who have come together to celebrate Mass ever since the Last Supper and with all those who will come after us until the end of time. As one of the Prefaces puts it:

> Earth unites with heaven
> to sing the new song of creation
> as we adore and praise you for ever.

The priest continues with this theme of thanksgiving and then prays that the Holy Spirit will come down on the gifts of bread and wine:

> And so, Father, we bring you these gifts.
> We ask you to make them holy by the power of your Spirit,
> that they may become the body and blood
> of your Son, our Lord Jesus Christ
> at whose command we celebrate this eucharist.

The central part of the Eucharistic Prayer recalls the events of that night when Jesus took bread and wine, blessed them and gave them to the apostles as his Body and Blood. At this moment we believe that, as the words of Jesus are said over them, the bread and wine become his body and blood. We proclaim our faith in Jesus now really present but still under the forms of bread and wine by singing another acclamation, such as:

> Christ has died.
> Christ is risen.
> Christ will come again.

You will notice that the acclamation is not just concerned with a past event, but with the present, and looks forward to the end of time. It is not only concerned with the Last Supper but with the whole story of our salvation – the fact that God loved us so much that he sent his Son to die for us, that he raised him up from the dead so that he is alive now and will come again to establish his kingdom of love, justice and peace at the end of time, when we shall be united with him and his Father.

The priest takes up this theme by recalling the passion, death and resurrection of Jesus and, looking forward to the end of time he offers the body and blood of Jesus to the Father so that

> all of us who share in the body and blood of Christ
> (may) be brought together in unity by the Holy Spirit.

The priest then prays for the needs of the Church and for the living and the dead. This is a salutary reminder that we are part of a community which stretches from earth to heaven, united in God's love.

The whole Eucharistic Prayer is concluded by praising God, as priest and people unite with Jesus in offering his body and blood to the Father:

> Through him,
> with him,
> in him,
> in the unity of the Holy Spirit,
> all glory and honour is yours,
> forever and ever

and the people make this offering their own by the acclamation, '*AMEN*'. Although Amen is a very short word, it is the most important of all the people's acclamations in the Mass because we are in fact saying 'yes' to all that has gone before. In the early days of Christianity, St Jerome was able to describe its sound as a thunderclap. St Augustine saw it as putting the people's seal on the Eucharistic Prayer. So, let us, too, sing or say Amen as if we really meant it, giving it the full weight of our assent.

God is our Father, a person in whom we can have absolute trust

CHAPTER 15

All creation gives you thanks and praise

Some thoughts on Eucharistic Prayer III

In this chapter, we shall look at Eucharistic Prayer III in some detail, considering the words and applying them to ourselves.

* * * * * *

Father

At this solemn moment in the Mass, we begin by addressing God as Father, just as Jesus taught us. God our Father is a person in whom we can have absolute trust; the most perfect of fathers, he loves all his children and seeks only what is good for them. Sometimes we may find it difficult to understand why some calamity has befallen us, but our faith helps us to see it as part of God's plan which we are unable, as yet, to understand; rather as a little child may not always understand why her mother and father say that she must do something. She does it because she knows that they love her and are caring for her.

Charles de Foucauld, who gave his life for the service of the poorest nomads in the Sahara Desert early in this century, put all this trust and dependency most beautifully in this prayer, which is known throughout the world as the Prayer of Abandonment:

> Father,
> I abandon myself into your hands,
> do with me what you will.
> Whatever you may do,
> I thank you.
> I am ready for all.

I accept all.
Let only your will be done in me
and all your creatures.
I wish no more than this, O Lord.
Into your hands I commend my soul;
I offer it to you with all the love of my heart,
for I love you, Lord, and so need to give myself,
to surrender myself into your hands, without reserve,
and with boundless confidence.
for you are my Father.

If we can make a prayer such as that our own then we shall have realised something of the Fatherhood of God and how close he is to us and we to him.

you are holy indeed,

The Eucharistic Prayer plunges us at once into the great mystery of God: he is our Father, but at the same time he is holiness itself. In him is all that is good and we can only be pale reflections of his holiness and goodness.

All the world knows Mother Teresa of Calcutta as a shining example of holiness and many already call her a saint, but although she is holy, she is still a human being with all a human being's imperfections. She is only able to do what she does because of God's help, as these extracts from a conversation with Malcolm Muggeridge show:

Mother Teresa If the work is looked at just by our own eyes and only from our own way, naturally, we ourselves can do nothing. But in Christ we can do all things. That is why this work is possible, because we are convinced that it is he, he who is working with us and through us in the poor and for the poor.
Malcolm The stimulus, the fire, the strength of what you are doing comes from that?
Mother Teresa It comes from Christ and the Sacrament.
Malcolm Which is why you begin each day with Mass?
Mother Teresa Yes, without him we could do nothing. And it is there at the altar that we meet our suffering poor. And in him that we see that suffering can become a means to a greater love, and greater generosity.*

*From *Something Beautiful for God*, Collins, 1971.

Mother Teresa is holy because of God's holiness and in God there are no imperfections. We thank God for people like Mother Teresa who by the holiness of their lives lead others to God, the source of all holiness.

and all creation rightly gives you praise.

God is our Father yet at the same time he is the creator of all that exists. The first book of the Bible, the Book of Genesis, emphasises this and in its story of the creation of our world shows God as the maker of all, well pleased with his work:

God saw all that he had made and indeed it was very good.

The story of the creation as recorded in Genesis was the product of a small nomadic tribe in an obscure desert on the edge of the then known civilisation and since it was set down in writing science has progressed. We now know a great deal about our planet earth and the myriads of plants and creatures, about the millions of planets and stars of the universe. It seems to me that the more we discover, the more we try to comprehend the incomprehensible distances which lie between us and the rest of the universe, the more we must realise that behind the universe there must be a mind, a creator, and we can only marvel that a God so great can love us and call us his children.

All life, all holiness comes from you
through your Son, Jesus Christ our Lord,
by the working of the Holy Spirit.

Our God is not some remote being, dwelling at the furthest end of the universe. He is a loving Father who communicates with us in the first place through his son, Jesus Christ, whom he sent to live on this little planet for thirty-three years or so, who died but rose from the dead and who, when he returned to the Father, sent the Holy Spirit to be his continuing presence here on earth with us.

It is as Christians, followers of Jesus, that we are called to bear witness to God's love for us and our faith in Jesus as

Lord gives us the strength and the courage to be Christians in a world which is becoming increasingly hostile or, worse, indifferent to the message of Jesus. To quote Mother Teresa once more:

. . . that is why we need the Eucharist, we need Jesus – to deepen our faith. If we can see Jesus in the appearance of bread, we can see him in the broken bodies of the poor. That is why we need that oneness with Christ, why we need that deep faith in Christ. It is very beautiful. When we have that deepening contact with Christ and can accept him fully, we can touch the broken bodies. We put it into practice straight away. You need the poor to touch him. You feed yourself in the Eucharist and after you are fed you want to use that energy, to give it out.*

The Holy Spirit is God's presence on earth. He lives within us and gives us the love and the courage to be followers of Jesus.

The world is still God's world. Christ has loved us and called us. The work he has begun, the Spirit will bring to completion. He has breathed his Spirit into us, gifted us with new capacities and intuitions.†

> *From age to age you gather a people to yourself,*
> *so that from east to west*
> *a perfect offering may be made*
> *to the glory of your name.*

The Bible is the story of a people, the Israelites, who believed that they were chosen by God to be his people; it is a record of how they turned from God and of how often he forgave them and welcomed them back again. This special relationship between God and his people was known as the covenant. A covenant was a sort of agreement, but much more. Gregory Manly in his book *At the table of the Lord* summarises it so:

*Quoted in Desmond Doig, *Mother Teresa, her people and her work*, Collins, 1976.
†E J Farrell STL, *Surprised by the Spirit*, Dimension Books, 1973.

(1) The initiative was God's not man's. [In other words, it was God who made the first approach.] (2) it brought about a special relationship in which the people were in fellowship with God [this is best expressed in the words: 'You shall be my people and I shall be your God.'] (3) the relationship would grow and find its final fulfilment only in the future; (4) the people had to live out the covenant by trusting in Yahweh [God] and in obedience to his will; and (5) the covenant is the sign of the origin of the Israelite nation.

The Israelites therefore looked forward to the coming of the Messiah who would establish God's kingdom. We believe that Jesus Christ was that Messiah who established not an earthly kingdom but a kingdom transcending time and space into which God has called his people from all over the world to be his children. The most perfect way in which we can be his children is by doing what he asked us to do on that last night of his life on earth. So we come together as God's people every Sunday to celebrate Mass together; to make the only perfect offering of which we are capable.

> *And so Father, we bring you these gifts.*
> *We ask you to make them holy by the power of your Spirit*
> *that they may become the body and blood*
> *of your Son, our Lord Jesus Christ,*
> *at whose command we celebrate this eucharist.*

In these few lines, we have a marvellous insight into the workings of God. To many the idea of the Holy Trinity – three Persons in one God – is very abstract, but here we see the Trinity in action in our lives.

God has made us; we owe our lives, our very existence to him and it is only right that we should offer to God our lives symbolised in the bread and wine.

But we are only human and nothing that we can give could, of itself, be worthy of being offered to the Father. We therefore call on the Holy Spirit to make them holy so that they are worthy of becoming the body and blood of the Lord Jesus who has commanded us to celebrate the eucharist, the Mass, until he comes again at the end of time.

In every sacramental celebration we call on the Holy Spirit, so that he may make God's word more fruitful in us. We ask him to help us encounter Christ. Above all, we ask him in the celebration of the Eucharist, at the moment of the consecration of the bread and wine, to make our offerings holy and to gather together into one body all those who receive.*

> *On the night he was betrayed,*
> *he took bread and gave you thanks and praise.*
> *He broke the bread, gave it to his disciples, and said:*
> *Take this, all of you, and eat it:*
> *this is my body which will be given up for you.*
> *When supper was ended, he took the cup.*
> *Again he gave you thanks and praise,*
> *gave the cup to his disciples, and said:*
> *Take this, all of you, and drink from it:*
> *this is the cup of my blood,*
> *the blood of the new and everlasting covenant.*
> *It will be shed for you and for all men*
> *so that sins may be forgiven.*
> *Do this in memory of me.*

And now we are taken back in time to that solemn evening when Jesus shared his last supper with his friends before he died on the cross. The priest takes the bread, says the words which Jesus used on that occasion, and the bread becomes the body of Christ. He takes the wine and again through the power of Christ's word, the wine becomes the blood of Christ. In doing this, the Church continues the tradition which St Paul recorded in his first letter to the Christians at Corinth:

For I received from the Lord the teaching that I passed on to you: that the Lord Jesus, on the night he was betrayed, took a piece of bread, gave thanks to God, broke it and said: 'This is my body, which is for you. Do this in memory of me.' In the same way, after supper he took the cup and said: 'This cup is God's new

*The Bishops of France, *Let us proclaim the mystery of faith*, Veritas Publications, 1980.

covenant, sealed with my blood. Whenever you drink it, do so in memory of me.'

This means that every time you eat this bread, and drink from this cup you proclaim the Lord's death until he comes.

St Ambrose, who was Bishop of Milan in Italy from 373 onwards, wrote this, of the power of God's word:

The word of Elijah had power to bring down fire from heaven; will not the word of Christ have power to change the nature of bread and wine? The sacrament you receive from the altar has been consecrated by the word of Christ himself. The words of institution are the actual words spoken by the Lord at the Last Supper. All the earlier parts of the Mass — the praise we offer God, the prayers the priest says for the people — all these are words of human origin; but when it comes to the consecration of the blessed sacrament, the priest no longer uses his own words but Christ's. The bread and wine are changed into the body and blood of Christ, therefore, by the word of Christ himself, the word by which all things were made.

Scripture tells us that the Lord spoke his word and the heavens were made; he spoke his word and the earth was made; he spoke his word and the seas were made; he spoke his word and every created thing came into existence. Jesus Christ is the Lord by whose word the whole universe was created. And if the word of the Lord Jesus has the power to create things out of nothing, surely it has the power to change existing things into something else. Before baptism you yourself belonged to the old creation, but once you were consecrated to God in the font you became a new creature. When he so desires, Christ can change anything in creation and the laws of nature themselves, simply by his word.

I want you to be absolutely sure of this teaching, to be convinced that the conversion of bread and wine into the Lord's body and blood is effected by words that are divine in origin.*

The priest shows us Christ's body and blood so that we may adore it in silence. These 'showings' of Christ's body and blood came into the Mass only in the thirteenth and late fourteenth century, when, unfortunately, people rarely received communion at all, because they felt that they

*Quoted in Anne Field OSB, *New Life*, Mowbray, 1980.

were too unworthy to do so. They had great satisfaction in just looking at the consecrated bread which was Christ's body. Today, thank God, we receive communion often, but this old custom is still retained in the Mass so that at this solemn moment, we may be united with the priest in adoring Jesus really present on the altar.

Then the priest invites us:

Let us proclaim the mystery of faith.

Our proclamation of faith is not something like:

Lord Jesus,
we adore you
truly present here on the altar

as it could well be. What we are actually asked to do is to 'proclaim the mystery of faith'. In other words, we are asked to profess our belief in the Lord Jesus, son of God, who lived, suffered, died and rose again from the dead, and is living now. He will come again at the end of time to establish his kingdom of love and peace. This mystery is expressed in the acclamations:

Christ has died,
Christ is risen,
Christ will come again.

Dying you destroyed our death,
rising you restored our life.
Lord Jesus, come in glory.

When you eat this bread and drink this cup,
we proclaim your death, Lord Jesus,
until you come in glory.

Lord, by your cross and resurrection
you have set us free.
You are the saviour of the world.

Notice how in all of them, we are taken from our present moment in time and linked with an event which took place in the past, but which is still present today.

In our gathering at worship, we have just recalled what God has done for us in Christ. We acknowledge his presence among us. We make it a point to dwell lovingly on what he is accomplishing among us. In the face of all the problems of our personal lives and in the world that would say nay, we assert that Christ indeed lives, risen, among us.

. . . as we proclaim that Christ has died, is risen, and will come again, we impress it on our consciousness. We become ever more aware each time of his saving power in our lives.*

> *Father, calling to mind the death your Son endured for our salvation,*
> *His glorious resurrection and ascension into heaven,*
> *and ready to greet him when he comes again,*
> *we offer you in thanksgiving this holy and living sacrifice.*

The priest takes up our acclamation and recalls the events of almost two thousand years ago, looking forward to the end of time, for which we now prepare by offering this 'holy and living sacrifice'. Sacrifice is a word which has lost its true meaning in our normal day-to-day use. If we have to do without something, however trivial, we talk of making a sacrifice. Sacrifice is all about having to give up something which is really precious to us, for the good of others, out of our love for them. The supreme sacrifice is to give up one's own life for the sake of another person – for instance, one often reads stories in the newspapers of mothers and fathers who risk and sometimes give their own lives, to save their children from fire, drowning, or some other danger.

One of the best examples in English fiction was Sydney Carton in Dickens' *A Tale of Two Cities* who died on the guillotine to save Charles Darnay:

It is a far, far better thing that I do, than I have ever done; it is a far, far better rest that I go to than I have ever known.

In our own times, the true story of Maximilian Kolbe is a perfect illustration of this great love which can raise

*Eugene S Geissler, Kenneth W Peters, *Together at Mass*, Indiana, USA, 1973.

human beings above even the terror and degradation of the concentration camps. Maximilian Kolbe was a Franciscan priest who was arrested by the Germans and sent to the notorious Auschwitz Concentration Camp. One day, after a prisoner had escaped, the Commandant decided to kill ten prisoners in retaliation. One of those chosen cried out that he would never see his wife and children again. Maximilian offered to exchange places with him, and his offer was accepted. Maximilian died of starvation, and the man he saved survived the war, and was present in St Peter's in Rome when Maximilian Kolbe was declared to be among the 'Blessed'.

The idea of sacrifice to the gods is an ancient one. Primitive people used to offer sacrifice to appease the gods or to ask for a good harvest. In some societies there was human sacrifice, but in the Jewish religion, animals were sacrificed – the 'first fruits' of a flock or herd.

Father Clifford Howell SJ in *The Work of our Redemption* describes the motives behind such sacrifices:

Human sacrifices seem to us very horrible; yet the idea behind them is all right. It is merely that the idea has become exaggerated; a perfectly sound instinct – to give to the god that which is most precious has become distorted. Some primitive people realised that human life is the most precious thing men have, and that is why they gave human life in sacrifice. Others, less primitive, realised that human life is not really theirs to dispose of, and so gave instead the life of some animal which was within their dominion. The life of the bull or goat and pig was meant to represent their own life. Or they gave things like food and drink which support human life. But the meaning was the same; they were saying in action: 'We want to give OURSELVES to you.'

Sacrifices in these rituals developed from a simple offering in which the victim was destroyed, into a sacred meal in which the victim was eaten. In other words, the victim (lamb, goat or bull) was offered to the god. The god accepted it, and then the people received their gift (or part of it) back again from the god, so that they could share it, as a sign that the god was pleased and wished to unite himself with them.

Jesus took the primitive idea and transformed it into the Mass. The event of the Last Supper did not end there. Under the form of bread and wine, Jesus offered his body and blood, but the next day on Calvary, he offered the sacrifice of his life to God, as he died the painfully cruel death of the cross. These two events are united in the celebration of Mass which is at one and the same time a sacred meal and the sacrifice of the cross. Jesus offered himself as a sacrifice to God to save the human race which had turned its back on God, and to restore it to God's friendship. This was the perfect sacrifice offered by Jesus who is truly God and truly man, and who had the power to lay down his life for our sakes. This was the one perfect sacrifice which achieved everything. No longer were sacrifices necessary because

Through Christ, God had at last the perfect worship which was his due; through Christ, in the person of Christ, man had at last offered the perfect sacrifice which effected the hitherto unachieved purpose of all sacrifices, namely the re-establishment of friendship between God and man. It made God and man 'at one' again and hence is called the 'at-one-ment'.*

When people talk of the priest offering the sacrifice of the Mass, we must realise that this is not a new sacrifice, but the one and same sacrifice which Jesus offered when he died on the cross. When we come to Mass, we are united with Jesus in that Black Friday, when the sun was darkened and the earth quaked and evil appeared to triumph over good. We now know that day as Good Friday, because it was Good which triumphed over Evil; this fact is celebrated by the Church in the Preface of the Triumph of the Cross:

Father, all-powerful and living God,
we do well always and everywhere to give you thanks.

*C Howell SJ, *The Work of our Redemption*, Fowler Wright Books.

You decreed that man should be saved through the wood of the
cross.
The tree of man's defeat became his tree of victory; where life
was lost, there life has been restored, through Christ our Lord.

and at the end of the Solemn Liturgy on Good Friday itself,
we have this prayer after communion:

> Almighty and eternal God
> you have restored us to life
> by the triumphant death and resurrection of Christ.
> Continue this healing work within us.
> May we who participate in this mystery
> never cease to serve you.

On the cross on that day Jesus offered his life to the Father
for us and won for us his friendship once more:

> God's love for us was revealed
> when God sent into the world his only Son
> so that we could have life through him;
> this is the love I mean:
> not our love for God,
> but God's love for us when he sent his Son
> to be the sacrifice that takes our sins away.
> My dear people
> since God has loved us so much,
> we too should love one another.
> (From the first letter of St John, chapter 4, verses 9–11)

> *Look with favour on your Church's offering*
> *and see the victim whose death has reconciled us to yourself.*
> *Grant that we who are united by his body and blood*
> *may be filled with his Holy Spirit*
> *and become one body, one spirit in Christ.*

Following on from all that has been said on sacrifice, we
ask the Father to accept our offering of the body and blood
of Jesus and ask him to fill us with the Holy Spirit so that
we may be united in Christ. You may have heard the
Church described as the Body of Christ, an idea which

goes back to St Paul who saw the Christian community as one body, with Christ at its head:

Christ is like a single body, which has many parts: it is still one body, even though it is made up of different parts. . . . All of you are Christ's body, and each one is a part in it (from St Paul's first letter to the Christians at Corinth).

As in any body, the parts must function together if the body is to work properly; so in Christ's body, the Church, all of us may have different parts to play, but we must work together if the Church is to function and bring people to know and love God.

The pope's title (or one of them anyway!) is 'Servant of the Servants of God' and this should really be the most important of all his titles, because if a Christian is to follow in the footsteps of Jesus, he must live a life of service. During the Last Supper which we have mentioned so often in this chapter, you will remember that Jesus got down on the floor and washed the feet of the apostles. This was not just a symbolic gesture – their feet would have been dusty and dirty – and Jesus did what slaves were expected to do. Afterwards, he explained his actions:

'Do you understand what I have done to you?' he asked. 'You call me Teacher and Lord, and it is right that you do so, because that is what I am. I, your Lord and Teacher, have just washed your feet. You, then, should wash one another's feet. I have set an example for you, so that you will do just what I have done for you. I am telling you the truth: no slave is greater than his master, and no messenger is greater than the one who sent him. Now that you know this truth, how happy you will be if you put it into practice!' (from the Gospel according to St John, chapter 13).

We are called to a life of service, to use our talents and gifts in God's service. In all that we do, we must be filled with love. As St Paul says,

I may have all the faith needed to move mountains – but if I have no love, I am nothing. I may give away everything I have, and even give my body to be burnt – but if I have no love, this does me no good (first letter to the Corinthians).

May he make us an everlasting gift to you
and enable us to share in the inheritance of your saints
with Mary, the virgin Mother of God;
with the apostles, the martyrs
and all your saints
on whose constant intercession we rely for help.

Now we are reminded of the Preparation of the Gifts, when we united our lives with the gifts which were brought forward to be later offered in sacrifice. As well as the bread and wine, our lives have been offered to God and we can become 'everlasting gifts' to God our Father. We are also reminded that we are not alone because the Church is much more than just the Church on earth. We are united with the Church in heaven, with Mary and with all the saints who are continually praying to God for us.

Lord, may this sacrifice,
which has made our peace with you,
advance the peace and salvation of all the world.
Strength in faith and love your
pilgrim Church on earth;
your servant Pope N., our Bishop N.,
and all the bishops,
with the clergy and the entire people your Son has gained for you.
Father, hear the prayers of the family you have gathered here
before you.
In mercy and love, unite all your children wherever they may be.

We pray now for the whole world, that all peoples may be saved. We pray for the Church in all the different countries of our world. We are a pilgrim Church because it is only at the end of time that we shall be perfectly united in the love of the Father. Till that time, the Church makes its way through the history of the world, subject to all the human failings of its members but, at the same time, strengthened 'in faith and love' by the Father who guides it in its mission to the world. So we remember all the members of that pilgrim Church on earth, the pope and our own bishop who has the care of the local diocese or Church in which we live. We remember our priests and all our brothers and sisters throughout the world and end by praying for the unity of all God's people.

> *Remember N.,*
> *in baptism he(she) died with Christ:*
> *may he(she) also share his resurrection,*
> *when Christ will raise our mortal bodies*
> *and make them like his own in glory.*
> *Welcome into your kingdom our departed brothers and sisters*
> *and all who have left this world in your friendship.*
> *There we hope to share in your glory*
> *when every tear will be wiped away.*
> *On that day we shall see you, our God, as you are,*
> *We shall become like you*
> *and praise you for ever through Christ our Lord*
> *from whom all good things come.*

In Masses for the Dead, this special, beautiful prayer may be added as we remember in a particular way all those who have died, our brothers and sisters in Christ, and we pray that they may be received into God's kingdom to live with him and the saints for all eternity. Of course, we pray for the dead every time we come to Mass, but this additional prayer brings out very clearly our faith in the resurrection of the dead. It is in fact referring to a passage in the book of the Apocalypse which in a way sums up all that the Mass is about – the sacrifice which makes us at one with God:

Then I saw a new heaven and a new earth. I heard a loud voice speaking from the throne: 'Now God's home is with mankind! He will live with them, and they shall be his people. God himself will be with them, and he will be their God. He will wipe away all tears from their eyes. There will be no more death, no more grief or crying or pain. The old things have disappeared (chapter 21).

Through him,
with him,
in him,
in the unity of the Holy Spirit,
all glory and honour is yours,
almighty Father,
for ever and ever.
Amen.

We come now to the grand finale of the Eucharistic Prayer. The priest raises the consecrated bread and wine as a gesture of offering and says a 'doxology', that is, a hymn in praise of God the Father, the Son, and the Holy Spirit, and the people make their this own by answering 'Amen'. This 'AMEN' is the most important of all the responses that we make at Mass; it is our personal assent to all that has taken place in the Eucharistic Prayer; it is our union of our lives with the body and blood of Jesus as they are offered to God our Father. We have heard how in the early Church this 'Great Amen' sounded like a crack of thunder. Unfortunately today we have a very rushed and muttered 'Amen', often obscured as we rise to say the Our Father. Priest and people should really treat this as a sacred moment; a moment when we say 'yes' to the work of our redemption accomplished by Jesus; when we acclaim the Father, the Son and the Holy Spirit for sharing with us their life.

Let our Amen be a real acclamation then; let it ring around the church like a thunderclap and let it ring in our hearts during the week when the church building is far away but the effects of the great Eucharistic Prayer, the Prayer of Thanksgiving, live on in our lives.

Part Four
We are Christ's body
The Rite of Communion

CHAPTER 16
Brothers and sisters of Jesus

With the sound of the Great Amen still ringing round the church, we stand (which in itself is a sign of joyful prayer) to prepare to receive Jesus in communion. The concern of the Church from now until communion is to emphasise our unity as children of God the Father, and brothers and sisters of Jesus.

We begin by calling God our Father; thereby acknowledging that all of us, no matter what our race or colour, are children of God and therefore belong with one another. The priest then prays for peace; we are reminded that we can only have peace in our world if first we have peace in ourselves and in our parish community. We therefore turn to one another and offer the peace of Christ with a sign of peace, which usually takes the form of a handclasp.

The priest takes the host and breaks it. This breaking is yet another sign of our unity because it echoes the words of Saint Paul:

The cup we use in the Lord's Supper and for which we give thanks to God: when we drink from it, we are sharing in the blood of Christ. And the bread we break: when we eat it, we are sharing in the body of Christ. Because there is one loaf of bread, all of us, though many, are one body, for we all share the one loaf (from the first letter to the Corinthians).

In most cases, we are unable to receive communion from one loaf of bread. But we can at least share in hosts consecrated at the same Mass and by this sharing, we have a sign, even if imperfect, of our unity.

The final sign of our unity in Christ is the actual receiving of communion. As a community, we come up to the altar and there we share in Christ's body and blood. Then in silence, as a community we pray to the Father giving thanks for the great gift of his Son whom we have received in communion.

. . . the result of receiving his body and blood is that God dwells in us more fully and we in him. This dwelling in one another brings a closeness which should continue and increase. It is measured by the strength of our faith and of our charity. The goal of this closeness is the vision of God, nothing less, in the fulness of glory after the resurrection. This is the goal, but it must begin here on earth.*

*Rene Voillaume, *Source of Life*, Darton, Longman & Todd, 1975.

CHAPTER 17

The prayer Jesus gave us

We are so used to saying the Our Father that we don't realise how beautiful a prayer it is, or how, each time we say it, we are challenging ourselves to be true followers of Jesus. Of all the prayers we use, it is the most specifically Christian since it was given to us by Jesus himself and sums up in some way all that his life was about.

In its directness and simplicity it has spoken to generations of Christians and shows the close relationship which Jesus wishes us to have with God. Sometimes people who write prayers or hymns try to stress the great awe we should have when speaking or singing to God. Thus, in the Orthodox Church, there is the hymn known as the Trisagion:

> O Holy God, O Holy and Mighty One,
> O Holy and Immortal, have mercy upon us.

This very beautiful hymn is an awesome reminder of the greatness and majesty of God, as is the Sanctus in our Mass:

> Holy, holy, holy Lord, God of power and might,
> heaven and earth are full of your glory.
> Hosanna in the highest.

Then there are the popular hymns such as:

> Immortal, invisible,
>   God only wise,
> In light inaccessible
>   hid from our eyes,
> most blessed, most glorious,
>   the Ancient of Days,
> almighty, victorious,
>   thy great name we praise.

Of course, as human beings, we must approach God with great love and reverence but when Jesus taught his followers how to pray this is what he said:

When you pray, do not use a lot of meaningless words, as the pagans do, who think that God will hear them because their prayers are long. Do not be like them. Your Father already knows what you need before you ask him. This, then, is how you should pray:
   Our Father in heaven:
   May your holy name be honoured;
   may your kingdom come;
   may your will be done on earth as it is in heaven.
   Give us today the food we need.
   Forgive us the wrongs we have done,
   as we forgive the wrongs that others have done to us.
   Do not bring us to hard testing,
   but keep us safe from the Evil One (from the Gospel of Matthew, chapter 6).

The word Jesus used for Father was the Aramaic word, *abba*, which is really a child's word for father, and the more correct translation would be 'daddy'. Our relationship with God is not to be one of fear but of love.

The Our Father comes at this part of the Mass because we are asking for our food, our 'daily bread' in the more familiar translation, which the Church links, of course, with the Bread of Life which we receive in communion. There is also the theme of forgiveness as we ask our Father to forgive us our failings and our sins, just as we forgive others. This is most appropriate as we prepare to receive communion, since it reminds us of our obligations to our neighbours. We shall be forgiven our sins only in so far as we are ready to forgive other people when they are in the wrong with us. At this point of the Mass, we can recall the warning of Jesus:

So if you are about to offer your gift to God at the altar and there remember that your brother has something against you, leave your gift there in front of the altar, go at once and make peace with your brother, and then come back and offer your gift to God (from the Gospel of Matthew, chapter 5).

In a few moments, we shall be asked to offer the sign of peace to one another; now is the time to consider if we are at peace with our family, our friends, our colleagues and if we are not, to resolve to make peace with them as soon as we can.

Above all, the Our Father is about praising God. Too often our prayers are 'prayers of petition', which really means that we are always asking God for things. We only have to think what in terms of our own human relationships we would think of a person who was always asking for things, to realise that if we are to have a genuine loving relationship with God our Father, we must in our prayers seek to build up that relationship. In all her prayers, the Church therefore begins by praising God and explains why in one of the Prefaces:

> You (Father) have no need of our praise,
> yet our desire to thank you is itself your gift.
> Our prayer of thanksgiving adds nothing to your greatness,
> but makes us grow in your grace,
> through Jesus Christ our Lord.

And so we praise God our Father, we pray that his kingdom will come, a kingdom of justice, love and peace, and by so praying we commit ourselves to working for the coming of that kingdom. We pray that God's will will be done on earth, just as it is in heaven. In all these ways, we are praising God and at the same time expressing our readiness to live out in our lives this close relationship which we have with the Father.

The Our Father ends and the priest takes up the last words *deliver us from evil* and embroiders them into a beautiful prayer asking God to give us peace, keep us free from sin, and protect us from all anxiety, *as we wait in joyful hope for the coming of our Saviour, Jesus Christ*.

Our response is another acclamation of praise which is

linked with our wish that God's kingdom may be established by the coming of Jesus:

> For the kingdom, the power and the glory are yours, now and for ever.

CHAPTER 18
Peace

Of all the changes in the Mass in recent years, perhaps the one people have had most difficulty in accepting is the Sign of Peace. Some said that it was because the English (or the Scots, the Irish, the Welsh, or the Americans) were too reserved and did not like to display their emotions in public, unlike the French or the Italians who gave the sign of peace much too enthusiastically – they actually looked as though they meant it! Some even kissed!

While there is some element of truth in this objection, perhaps the real reason is that at this point of the Mass, the time for talking is over. It is marvellous to say that we love our neighbour, but do we have the courage to turn to him or her, shake hands and say, *Peace be with you*? Action is required as well as words, and the sign of peace is a reminder to us of just how short we are on actions in our lives. At Church on Sunday, we may be happy to call ourselves Christians and think with love of our brothers and sisters throughout the world, but when it comes to doing something positive to help them we find all sorts of excuses to avoid our responsibilities. As St James tell us in his letter:

My brothers, what good is it for someone to say he has faith if his actions do not prove it? Can that faith save him? Suppose there are brothers and sisters who need clothes and don't have enough to eat. What good is there in your saying to them, 'God bless you! Keep warm and eat well!' – if you don't give them the necessities of life. So it is with faith: if it is alone and includes no actions, then it is dead.

The Hebrew word for peace is *shalom* and its meaning goes beyond our own word – it means all possible

Action is required as well as words. The sign of peace is a reminder of just how short we are on actions in our lives

prosperity, the state of a person in complete harmony with himself, with the world around him and with God. When we say, *Peace be with you*, we are praying that the peace of Christ will be with our neighbour; that Christ himself will be always with him, guiding him in all that he does. It is a sign of love for one another as God's people gathered together and a sign of our unity as brothers and sisters in Christ.

Although it is new to us, the sign of peace is in fact a very ancient part of the Mass. Among the early Christians, it was seen as a seal placed on their prayer. It has had various places in the Mass. At first, it followed the prayer of the faithful, and at this point it could be seen as a sign of love, before the gifts were offered at the altar. Later on it was moved to a position immediately after the Our Father by Pope Innocent I who said that it was 'a sign of the people's acquiescence in all that has been done in these mysteries'. It has followed the Our Father's petition that we be forgiven 'as we forgive those who trespass against us'. Eventually, it came to be closely linked with the receiving of Christ's body in communion and as with the passage of time fewer and fewer people actually received communion at Mass, so the sign of peace came to be reserved only to those who were on the Sanctuary and even there it became highly formalised.

Today the sign of peace is given in most churches at most Masses and is exchanged by those who are near to one another. The custom of the priest coming from the sanctuary and giving it to the people is one that the Church rather frowns on, since it is not really intended that the 'peace' should be something which comes from the celebrant; it is an expression of the love and peace that exists within the community assembled in God's name.

Although it has been a little slow to catch on in some places, the sign of peace is now exchanged with love and enthusiasm in many parishes. I have heard how impressed are visitors from other denominations at the sign of peace. Suddenly they feel a part of the assembly; the bitterness of division begins to crumble as Christians look at one another and exchange this ancient sign of their mutual love.

CHAPTER 19
One in Christ

And the bread we break: when we eat it, we are sharing in the body of Christ. Because there is one loaf of bread, all of us, though many, are one body, for we all share the one loaf (from the first letter of St Paul to the Christians at Corinth).

They (the Christians) went as a body to the Temple every day but met in their houses for the breaking of bread . . . (from the Acts of the Apostles).

One of the most beautiful stories in the New Testament concerns the experience of the two disciples of Jesus after the crucifixion. Broken-hearted, they were making their way back to their home town of Emmaus. As they were walking along, a man joined them and asked what they were talking about. One of them, Cleopas, answered with some asperity: 'You must be the only person staying in Jerusalem who does not know the things that have been happening there these last few days.' He then tells the stranger of the death of Jesus on the cross, and how rumours were now beginning to circulate that the women had found the tomb empty and had 'seen a vision of angels who declared that he was alive'. The stranger then began to explain the passages in scripture that were about Jesus.

St Luke takes up the story:

When they drew near to the village to which they were going, he made as if to go on; but they pressed him to stay with them. 'It is nearly evening' they said 'and the day is almost over.' So he went in with them. Now while he was with them at table, he took the bread and said the blessing; then he broke it and handed it to them. And their eyes were opened and they recognised him; but he had vanished from their sight.

They immediately hurried back to the Apostles at Jerusalem; and they told their story of what had happened on the road and how they had recognised him at the breaking of the bread.

One of the earliest names for what we now know as the Mass, was the Breaking of the Bread, because it was in the breaking and distribution of the bread that Christians were united with their risen Lord. They recognised Jesus in the breaking of the bread; the sharing in the one loaf was a vivid reminder of their unity in Christ. As with many of the signs and symbols of the Mass, we have allowed this very powerful sign of our union in Christ as Body to be diminished: now instead of using one loaf, we use small discs which look more like plastic than bread, the actual breaking being confined to the priest's large host. He breaks this and drops a particle of it into the chalice as a sign of the re-uniting of Christ's body and blood; a sort of symbol of the resurrection!

This wouldn't be quite so bad, were it not for the other unfortunate custom of using hosts consecrated at a previous Mass to give communion to the people. This practice has been condemned by successive popes, but it continues, destroying the idea that the people take part fully in the offering of the Mass which they are attending. In addition, the Church is strongly encouraging the use of bread which really looks and tastes like bread.

It would be easy to get lost in these criticisms of the way Mass is celebrated, and to forget the real purpose of this breaking of the bread, which is to show vividly our unity in Christ's body – and not only the unity of the congregation present in the church, but the unity of the whole Church, of all the men and women for whom Christ died on the cross.

The theme of the 1981 Eucharistic Congress in Lourdes was: 'The Eucharist – Jesus Christ, bread broken for a new world'. Pope John Paul II writing to those taking part in the Congress said:

It was really, in fact, in order that mankind would not shut itself up in its refusal, that injustice should not have the last word; that hatred should be abolished and that history should open for a new future, that Christ agreed to be on the cross himself the victim offered for sin, unbelief and injustice. It was at that hour that he, the living Bread come down from heaven, carried out on our earth the breaking of bread par excellence by spreading his hands freely on the cross in order to destroy death and lead to life.

Father Tissa Balasuriya in his book *The Eucharist and Human Liberation** emphasises the need for us to realise our unity with our brothers and sisters throughout the world:

We may ask ourselves how it is possible that societies calling themselves Christian can offer the Eucharist weekly, for years, without improving the relationships among persons in it. What would be the meaning of fifty-two Masses offered during a year in a city if as a result of it there were no effort at bridging the immense gulf that separates the rich in their mansions and the poor in their shanties? Is not the Eucharist a part of the sacrament of unity? St Paul himself complained bitterly that those who participated in the Eucharist were not tending towards unity. 'If you receive the body and blood of Christ unworthily, do you not receive judgement unto yourself?'

It was such an understanding of the Eucharist that made Paul critical of the abuses that were creeping in among the Corinthians even in those early days. He wanted the Eucharist to be a real sharing in mind and goods and therefore he says that the Eucharistic community is to form one body: 'When we break the bread, is it not a means of sharing the body of Christ? Because there is one loaf, we, many as we are, are one body; for it is one loaf of which we all participate' (1 Cor. 10:16–17). He continues; 'Anyone who eats the bread or drinks the cup of the Lord unworthily will be guilty of desecrating the body and blood of the Lord' (1 Cor. 11:27).

*SCM Press, 1979.

CHAPTER 20

The Lamb of God

St John in the first chapter of his Gospel describes the first meeting between Jesus and John the Baptist:

The next day, seeing Jesus coming towards him, John said, 'Look, there is the lamb of God that takes away the sin of the world. This is the one I spoke of when I said: A man coming after me who ranks before me because he existed before me' . . . John also declared, 'I saw the Spirit coming down on him from heaven like a dove and resting on him. . . . Yes, I have seen and I am the witness that he is the Chosen One of God.'

Why call Jesus the Lamb of God? In doing so, John was prophesying the death of Jesus because the lamb was the animal which the Jews sacrificed in their passover feast when they celebrated the night of their rescue from Egypt where they were held in slavery; the night the angel of death passed over the houses marked with the blood of the lamb.

In the Book of Revelation, St John has a vision of Jesus as the Lamb of God, who has taken away the sins of the world:

One of the elders then spoke, and asked me 'Do you know who these people are, dressed in white robes, and where they have come from?' I answered him, 'You can tell me, my Lord.' Then he said, 'These are the people who have been through the great persecution, and because they have washed their robes white in the blood of the Lamb, they now stand in front of God's throne and serve him day and night in his sanctuary' (chapter 7).

Now, at this point in the Mass, while the priest is breaking the bread, we sing a hymn, the Lamb of God, in which we pray that Jesus the Lamb of God, will have mercy on us and grant us peace.

The priest then raises the consecrated bread which is the Body of Christ and says:

> This is the Lamb of God
> who takes away the sins of the world.
> Happy are those who are called to his supper.

The supper to which this invitation refers is also mentioned in the Book of Revelation in which the marriage of the lamb and God's Church takes place as a symbol of the beginning of the heavenly kingdom:

'Alleluia! The reign of the Lord our God Almighty has begun; let us be glad and joyful and give praise to God, because this is the time for the marriage of the Lamb. His bride is ready, and she has been able to dress herself in dazzling white linen, because her linen is made of the good deeds of the saints.' The angel said, 'Write this: Happy are those who are invited to the wedding feast of the Lamb.'

Our reply to this invitation is:

> Lord, I am not worthy to receive you,
> but only say the word and I shall be healed.

This brings to our minds an incident in Matthew's Gospel:

When Jesus went into Capernaum, a centurion came up and pleaded with him. 'Sir,' he said, 'my servant is lying at home, paralysed, and in great pain.' 'I will come myself and cure him,' said Jesus. The centurion replied, 'Sir, I am not worthy to have you under my roof; just give the word and my servant will be cured' (chapter 8).

When we say this prayer we are acknowledging our sinfulness. We know that no one is worthy to stand before God, but the important feature of this prayer is not our unworthiness, but our faith in the love of God who loves us even though we are sinners. Faith can work wonders and at this point of the Mass, when we are about to receive Jesus in communion, we express our faith in God who loves us enough to give us so great a gift.

CHAPTER 21

We are Christ's body

We gave grown up with the idea that communion is a very personal moment; the time when 'I' receive 'my' Lord Jesus under the form of bread; the time of silent communion with 'my' Lord. It is certainly that, but it is much more.

The whole of the Communion Rite from the Our Father to this moment has been emphasising our unity as brothers and sisters in Christ. It would be strange if, at this moment, when we are to receive him in communion, we should destroy that unity by behaving as individuals, unconcerned for our brothers and sisters.

When we come up to communion, we come up as a procession, and this procession is united by the Communion Song which, like all the music of the Mass, should bring us together as God's people.

We stand before the priest or the minister of communion, and we are asked to make our own profession of faith in Jesus really present. The host is held in front of us, as the minister says: The Body of Christ. Our response, *Amen* (which you will remember means 'So be it') is an act of faith. This is a most important moment for each one of us and should not be rushed either by ourselves or by the minister.

Once, it was the normal practice for all present at Mass to receive communion under the forms of bread and wine. After all, this was the Lord's solemn command at the Last Supper on the night before he died – Take and eat; Take and drink. It is unfortunate that, with the passage of time, communion under both kinds for the laity became increasingly rare. Of course, Jesus is really present under the form of bread or of wine alone, but since the Mass is a sacred banquet, it loses much of the symbolism of a meal if we are not able to drink. Wine is after all a sign of joy. It transforms an ordinary meal into a special one, and unites us more closely with the events of that Last Supper when Jesus gave us his flesh to eat and his blood to drink. In our days, we are seeing a return to the ancient custom of receiving communion under both kinds.

Having received Christ, we return to our places, perhaps still singing. After the hymn, a blessed silence ought to descend on the church as we all join together in silent prayer. United in this silence, we may well pray for ourselves, but are much more likely to pray for others: the dead members of our families who used to kneel beside us in our church; the sick who are not with us; the poor and the suffering, and those who do not believe. We give thanks too that Jesus has come to us in this special way; to unite us with himself and with the Father, and is gradually transforming our lives so that we may become more faithful Christians.

Our communion in the sacrament of the body and blood of Jesus helps to bring about this transformation. We are not merely united to Christ by faith, we must also be transformed into him by love, love with all its difficulty. We cannot make this transformation ourselves, we can do nothing without Christ's grace and communion in him. So the sacrament of the eucharist is above all the sacrament of love, and that unity which is the fruit of love. . . . The Fathers often pointed out that bread is formed from many grains of wheat and wine is made from many grapes, which is a natural symbol for the unity of the Christian people.*

The communion rite finishes with a prayer after communion in which we thank God for the wonderful gift we have received, and pray that it may influence our lives, e.g.

> Lord, you have nourished us with bread from heaven.
> Fill us with your Spirit
> and make us one in peace and love.

*Rene Voillaume, *Source of Life*, Darton, Longman and Todd, 1975.

Part Five

TO LOVE AND SERVE THE LORD

The Mass in our lives

CHAPTER 22

To love and serve the Lord

We come now to the end of Mass. The priest blesses us and sends us out into the world. When the Mass was in Latin, the priest would say: 'Ite missa est.' *Missa* was a Latin word for dismissal and signified the breaking up of a meeting. From the fourth century onwards, it gave its name to the whole celebration and in English, 'Missa' became 'Mass'. This is therefore a most important moment in the Mass and the Order of Mass as we now have it makes this quite clear, especially in the words,

> Go in peace to love and serve the Lord.

The Mass does not end when we go out of the Church door. During our celebration we have been given the necessary strength to go out into the world to preach Christ – to proclaim the Gospel with our lives.

One of the principal reasons for the many empty Christian churches today is that there are too many Sunday Christians whose Christianity is limited to an hour in church on Sunday mornings. The true follower of Jesus will try to live out his faith all through the week, in all the different circumstances he or she meets, at home, in the office, shop or classroom, or on the factory floor. Christians are called to bear witness to Christ's love for all by the love they show to one another, and their neighbours who may not know Christ. It was possible to say of the early Christians 'See, how they love one another', but could that be said of us now? As one of the Wayside Pulpits has it: 'If you were arrested for being a Christian, would there be enough evidence to convict you?'

We ought to remember that Christians are not called to an easy life. Our vocation is to be witnesses to Christ and to bring him to those who do not know him. It may involve us in great sacrifices; it may mean that we have to give up things that we love, but above all, we have to remember that Christianity is about people; about bringing God's message to the poorest and most abandoned.

When we come to church on Sundays to worship God, we do so to the best of our ability. We build beautiful churches and make beautiful music, have beautiful vestments and flowers; all of which are important signs of our love and reverence for God. If that love and reverence stop there, we are failing to live to the full our Christian lives.

St John Chrysostom expresses it very pungently:

Do you want to honour Christ's body? Then do not scorn him in his nakedness, nor honour him here in the church with silken garments while neglecting him outside where he is cold and naked. For he who said: 'This is my body', and made it so by his words, also said: 'You saw me hungry and you did not feed me,' and 'inasmuch as you did it for one of these, the least of my brothers, you did it for me.' What we do here in the church requires a pure heart, not special garments; what we do outside requires great dedication.

Of what use is it to weigh down Christ's table with golden cups, when he himself is dying of hunger? First, fill him when he is hungry; then use the means you have left to adorn his table. Will you have a golden cup made but not give a cup of water? What is the use of providing the table with cloths woven of gold thread and not providing Christ himself with the clothes he needs?

Once again, I am not forbidding you to supply these adornments; I am urging you to provide these other things as well, and indeed to provide them first. No one has ever been accused for not providing ornaments, but for those who neglect their

neighbour a hell awaits with an inextinguishable fire and torment
in the company of the demons. Do not, therefore, adorn the
church and ignore your afflicted brother, for he is the most
precious temple of all.*

If tomorrow our country were to become an atheist state
and all the church buildings, all our magnificent Cathe-
drals, were to be closed down, the Church would still live
on in the hearts, minds and actions of Christians who
would continue to meet together in secret to celebrate the
eucharist together, just as Christians in past ages have
done. Jesus has told us that what God requires from his
followers is worship in spirit and in truth, and for that we
do not need the magnificence of our church buildings.
Indeed, some people would argue that the very magnificence of these buildings is contrary to Christ's teaching,
especially in a world where the poor have nowhere to live
and nothing to eat.

   What we must have, as committed Christians, is love for
God and love for our neighbours whoever and wherever
they may be, at whatever cost. Today in a world seemingly
intent on its own destruction, this witness is needed more
than ever. If we fail to give it, we are not putting into
practice what we say and do in church. As you go from the
church building next Sunday to love and serve the Lord,
remember that you are called to take Jesus with you into
your world, to make it his world once more.

*From a homily on St Matthew by St John Chrysostom, taken from the
Liturgy of the Hours in the ICEL translation.

CHAPTER 23

The sound of music

It would be a strange world if we didn't have music. Can you imagine life without the sound of any music – no Beethoven, no Beatles! It would be dull, flat and lifeless; music adds a completely new dimension to our daily life. It would be like living in a world without colour.

Can you imagine how the words of a pop song would sound if they didn't have music? There is a very funny record of Peter Sellers reading the words of 'A hard day's night' in the style of Laurence Olivier. All the zest, all the life of the original song is lost.

It wouldn't do if everything were to be sung, of course. Great poetry and great prose exist without any help from music since their beauty lies in their language. *King Lear* would gain nothing from being set to music! But music can add a new dimension in some cases. The beautiful settings by Schubert of poems by great poets such as Goethe and Schiller and even Shakespeare blended his genius with theirs to create masterpieces loved throughout the world. Music can take the spoken word and transform it, giving it new life and new meaning.

The same applies to the use of music in church. There are some parts of the Mass which are best spoken and there are others which cry out to be sung. The Mass is a celebration of our faith and the use of music can help us to deepen that faith, and to proclaim it in a particular way – rousing and joyful, or solemn and sad. Music can set the whole mood for a celebration and it would be good if we could have some music at each of the Masses on Sunday. It doesn't have to be elaborate; it can just be simple, direct yet still beautiful.

Unfortunately, there seems to be a reluctance to sing in our churches today – another un-English activity? Gradu-

Music can set the whole mood of a celebration

ally, however, we are coming to realise how good it is to be able to sing at Mass and how much is added to our celebration. Perhaps, one day we shall capture the fervour of the great Welsh choirs we hear on 'Songs of Praise' or at Cardiff Arms Park.

What should we sing?

There are certain very important parts of the Mass which ought to be sung if at all possible.

The Acclamations
These are the acclamation before the Gospel; the Holy, holy; the acclamation after the consecration of the Body and Blood of Jesus in the Eucharistic Prayer; and the Great Amen at the end of the Eucharistic Prayer. Acclamations are, or should be, great shouts of joy. While they can be said, their full beauty and power are brought out if they are sung.

The Responsorial Psalm
Psalms are for singing and it makes as much sense to say most of the psalms as it would to say a pop song. It's really quite easy to sing the psalm; all that is needed is a good singer to sing the verse and to lead the people in singing a simple response to each verse.

The Songs of the Mass
These are the Lord have mercy (*Kyrie*); Glory to God (*Gloria*); and Lamb of God (*Agnus Dei*) which are very ancient parts of a sung Mass. They are songs which belong to the whole congregation to help them pray to God.

Hymns
Most people like singing hymns. At Mass there may be hymns at the Entry, the Offertory and Communion processions, and at the end. The hymns should be chosen to

bring out the theme of the readings at the Mass and to re-inforce their message.

Priest's chants
At special Masses, the priest may also sing other parts of the Mass, such as 'The Lord be with you', with a simply sung people's response. This adds extra dignity to the celebration of Mass.

Who should sing?

The answer to that question is simple: everyone! Everyone should try to sing at Mass as a sign of our joy; it unites us emotionally, making us feel that we really are one people, a community at prayer.

To help us in our singing, we have choirs who lead us in the praise of God and sometimes sing special items on their own, or they may provide descants or harmonies for the parts of the Mass which the congregation is singing.

What music do we sing?

The music used in the Church has varied from age to age. In the early persecuted Church, there was no music at all since the sound of music would have led to the detection of these secret gatherings and when it came to be introduced, there was some reluctance. St Augustine, a great bishop who lived in the fourth century, was particularly worried that he might be tempted to take too much pleasure in the music rather than the words and wondered if music should be banned from churches. However, he concluded:

Yet when I remember the tears I shed, moved by the songs of the Church in the early days of my new faith; and again when I see that I am moved not by the singing but by the things that are sung – when they are sung with a clear voice and proper modulation – I recognise once more the usefulness of this practice.

Yet whenever it happens that I am more moved by the singing than the thing sung, I admit that I have grievously sinned, and then I should wish rather not to have heard the singing.*

For a long part of the Church's history, the music used was settings of Latin words. This music was in various styles from the austere beauty of plainsong, which developed to the intricate beauty of polyphony created by composers such as Monteverdi. Some of the greatest music by the greatest composers has been settings of the Latin Mass. These have really been more suited to the concert hall than to the church because of their length and the high standards of musicianship needed to perform them.

Today, with our new liturgy in English we are slowly producing settings of the Mass which are designed for congregations and choirs to sing. Some of these are quite traditional, and others are in the folk tradition. Our repertoire of hymns is also being increased by modern hymns written in various styles.

In many parishes you will find on a typical Sunday a 'traditional' Mass sung in Latin or English by choir and congregation, and accompanied by an organ; a family Mass using a simple English setting; and a Folk Mass with folk hymns. The style is not important: what is important is that the music should be good, in its own way; that it should be sung well by congregation and choir; above all, that it helps us to pray.

If we never had singing at Mass, we should be missing a great deal. We could still hear God's word and still receive communion, but we should be losing the whole idea of joyful praise. When we are happy it is natural to sing and if we don't sing at Mass, we don't show forth the joy which the Mass brings us. 'Song is for joy – even hidden in sorrow – and joy is praise.'†

When we sing at Mass, we sing with joy of the great love

*St Augustine, *Confessions*, book X, Chapter 33.
†Hildelith Cumming OSB, *Music for Evening Prayer*, Collins, 1977.

God has for us. Our voices unite in prayer and help us to become a people united in praise of God and his love. Music, the food of that love, nourishes us and brings us closer to God.

CHAPTER 24
The sound of voices

The sound of voices – voices raised in anger; voices full of love; voices full of bitterness; lonely voices pleading for help; voices of children playing: wherever we go, we hear voices as people communicate with one another and get to know one another. The wildlife broadcaster, David Attenborough, has described mankind as 'the compulsive communicators':

Man's passion to communicate and receive communications seems as central to his success as a species as the fin was to the fish or the feather to the birds. We do not limit ourselves to our own acquaintances or even our own generation. Archaeologists labour to decipher clay tablets rescued with painstaking care from Uruk and other ancient cities in the hope that some citizen long ago may have recorded a message of more significance than a boastful genealogy of a chief or a laundry list. In our own cities dignitaries arrange for messages to be sent to future generations by burying writings in steel cylinders strong enough to survive even a nuclear catastrophe. And scientists, convinced that man's most refined language is mathematics, select a universal truth that they believe will be recognised through all eternity – a formula for the wavelength of light – and beam it towards other galaxies in the Milky Way to proclaim that here on earth, after three thousand million years of evolution, a creature has emerged that has for the first time devised its own way of accumulating and transferring experience across generations.*

Compulsive communicators we may be, but it seems that one of the great problems of our age is that we don't listen:

> And in the naked light I saw
> Ten thousand people, maybe more;
> People talking without speaking;
> People hearing without listening. †

*Life on earth, Collins, 1979.
†Simon and Garfunkel, 'The Sound of Silence'.

In church we are surrounded by voices and we ought to listen to them since they will help us to come together as God's People. Perhaps the first voice we hear is the voice of the usher welcoming us to the church with a cheerful 'Good Morning!'; helping us to feel part of this community and not just an individual among strangers.

There is the voice of the priest celebrating the Mass: welcoming us to the celebration; leading us in prayer and perhaps proclaiming the Gospel; speaking to us of God in the homily; saying the Eucharistic Prayer and, by God's power, making present the Body and Blood of Jesus as our food and drink.

There is the voice of the reader who reads the scriptures in church. He or she is a servant of God's word and a servant of the community. As a servant of God's word, the reader must set out to interpret faithfully the message contained in the scripture readings. He can only serve the word by preparing by study and prayer to read it. He must proclaim the word with faith and understanding, always aware that God is speaking to his people through him. As a servant of the community, the reader must try to inspire them to listen carefully to his voice as he shares with them God's message. The last words he speaks are very important: 'This is the word of the Lord' – in these words he is asking us to profess our faith as a community that the Lord has spoken to us in the readings, that we have heard his voice.

There is the voice of the choir, leading us in singing God's praises. Sometimes it will sing pieces of music on its own, to help us to meditate on some particular aspect of our celebration. There is the voice of the cantor, who sings the Responsorial Psalm and sometimes helps us to sing our parts of the Mass.

There is the voice of the special minister of communion during the distribution of holy communion, serving the congregation by his or her ministry so that they may receive communion in a dignified and unhurried way. When he speaks to us, his voice asks us to profess our faith in Jesus really present under the forms of bread and wine. As we shall see in a later chapter, his voice will be heard by the sick of the parish as he brings the Body of the Lord from the community gathered in church to the sick in their homes.

We don't hear the voices of the altar servers (or we shouldn't) because their job in the celebration of Mass is essentially practical – to make sure that the priest has everything he needs as he needs it. Their presence lends beauty and dignity to the celebration.

Finally, but perhaps most important, there is the voice of the community raised in prayer and song – many voices united in the praise of God; praying together and listening to other voices as they lead us in worship. The voice of the community is a vital part of the celebration of Mass: the community listens and responds to God's word; the community joins with the priest in offering the sacrifice of the Mass: 'Pray, brothers and sisters, that our sacrifice may be acceptable to God the almighty Father.' The community joins with the priest in thanking God in the Eucharistic Prayer by listening to the prayer and making it its own by the acclamations within the prayer; the community prepares as one body to receive Jesus in communion; and it is as a living community that we are sent out to love and serve the Lord.

Why are our voices important? Why should we take an active part in the liturgy? Liturgy is from a Greek word which meant an act of public service and it was at first used by Christians to describe any act of service or ministry to the community. Gradually it came to be applied only to service to God and then, since worship is the supreme service of God, it was applied to the Mass and to the other sacraments of the Church.

Liturgy is the public worship of God by the whole Church. It is not just the concern of the priest, choir, and servers but of each member of the whole Christian people who take an active part in the celebration of Mass, not just by their voices, but by their silent prayer, by listening to

God's word, and by their actions during Mass – standing to pray, joining in processions, and so on.

By our baptism we were given the right to take part in the Mass and it is a very precious right since in the Mass we meet Jesus in a very special and intimate way. We were also given the duty to take our part, and this means that we have to involve the whole of our lives in the preparation for, and in the celebration of the Mass.

I wish briefly to reaffirm the fact that Eucharistic worship constitutes the soul of all Christian life. In fact, Christian life is expressed in the fulfilling of the greatest commandment, that is to say in the love of God and neighbour, and this love finds its source in the Blessed Sacrament, which is commonly called the sacrament of love.*

Voices not heard often enough are the voices of the children of the parish. Some people talk of them as the 'Church of tomorrow' but this isn't true: they are the Church of today, just as much as you and I, and have a right to take part in the Mass to the full extent of their capabilities. That is why the Church issued a special Directory on Children's Masses and encouraged parishes to do their best to help children take their full part in the Mass. Some parishes have Children's Masses, or a special Liturgy of the Word for children. Others have Family Masses in which the children are encouraged to take a prominent part – reading the scriptures, announcing the intentions in the Prayer of the Faithful, bringing up the gifts of bread and wine at the Offertory, leading the singing. In these and other ways, children can be made to feel a part of the community and will grow up knowing the Mass as something beautiful and interesting, not something dull and boring!

The final words we hear are from the priest: 'Go in peace,' he says, 'to love and serve the Lord.' We love and serve the Lord by taking his voice into our world, because

*Pope John Paul II, *Letter on the Holy Eucharist.*

we are the voices of the Lord to those of our neighbours who know us as Christians. Our lives proclaim the Lord's Good News bringing his love and care to our world, but we must be ready to listen to his voice, and to the voices of those who need us.

```
. . .but to listen
              to listen intently
my God i wish i could listen
                    to my brother
listen to his heart beats
listen to those faint . . . o so faint . . .
                    calls
                    which are there
                    hidden
under . . . i know not why . . .
          some sort of fear
listening
          but instead
            i have my own ideas
            and i penetrate
               destroying
               harvesting all that is there
to make bread
               for i
               for me
               for myself. *
```

*Jean Vanier, *Tears of Silence*, Darton, Longman and Todd, 1970.

CHAPTER 25

The sound of silence

We live in a very noisy world. Everywhere there seems to be noise – cars, buses, aeroplanes, transistors, televisions, and the inevitable piped music. Even the most peaceful places seem to have been invaded by noise.

When we go to church even, we have the distinct impression of being talked at from beginning to end. My inevitable reaction to being talked *at* is not to listen! At one time we had a silent liturgy; the silence being disturbed only by the murmur of the priest saying 'his' Mass and the hurried and inaudible responses of the altar server. Some older people look back to this time with longing but it was not, of course, the ideal. Instead of following the Mass, the majority of the congregation got on with their own private devotions such as the Rosary, or prayers about the Mass. Only a few tried to 'follow the Mass' in their Missals and I can remember how, as a boy, I was pleased if I managed to keep up with the priest and get to the Consecration at the same time as he did. But we come to church to worship together, in unison with one another and the priest, and it is only right that we should be able to hear and understand the prayers which the priest says on our behalf, and to pray aloud with one another. It is for this reason that all the principal prayers of the Mass are said aloud. However, the Church recognises the need for silence in the Mass, and strongly recommends it. There should be periods of silence at various parts of the Mass:

At the Penitential Rite: Here we should be given time to be recollected and to think of our failures to follow Jesus so that we may ask his forgiveness.

At the Opening Prayer: Again we should have the opportunity to think of what the priest will pray about on our behalf.

At the end of the readings and the homily: The pauses for silence should allow us to meditate briefly on what we have heard.

During the prayer of the faithful: there should be a silent pause after each petition to allow us to make the petition our own, and there is also a time for silent prayer for our own intentions before the priest says the final prayer of the prayer of the faithful.

After communion: here the Church asks us to praise God in our hearts and to pray. This is a most solemn time and we should take this opportunity to unite ourselves more closely with Jesus whom we have just received.

In addition the Pope has encouraged us to come a little early to Mass to prepare ourselves to join in the celebration of Mass, and to stay for a while at the end to make our own personal thanksgiving.

People sometimes think of silent prayer as private prayer and cannot see how necessary it is that there should be times during the Mass for the whole community to pray silently together. There is something strangely impressive about a large gathering of people completely silent, completely still. Within that community, individuals will be praying for their own intentions but all these different intentions will be gathered up in one great silent prayer to the Father. Every year in November the two-minute silence is kept throughout the country as we remember those who died fighting for their country and, if you have ever been at the Cenotaph Ceremony in London you will know how moving and how impressive is the silence which descends on the city as Big Ben strikes eleven and the guns boom in Hyde Park.

Silence, as they say, is golden and we need more of it in

We offer silent prayers as individuals, but also as a part of the community

our celebration of Mass if we really are to make the Mass our own. But we need to be educated once more in the use of silence so that we spend the time in meditation on the particular part of the Mass and not wondering if 'Father' has forgotten what he was going to do next. It is one of the functions of the priest to lead us in our silent prayer and if, by his own actions, he can give us an example of silent, meditative prayer then we will more easily learn how to pray in silence; to meditate on the readings and prayers and really make them our own. Eventually we shall reach the stage when silent prayer comes naturally and there is an easy flow between the public prayers said aloud by priest and people and the silent prayer which we offer as individuals but also as part of a community.

The final stage in any human relationship is the moment when words become an actual hindrance to communication. They get in the way because they cannot express what one wants to express. Only silence can do that. It is not an empty silence, but a silence charged with rich meaning like a thundercloud heavy with rain.*

When boy meets girl and they start to go out with each other, they talk a lot as they try to discover more about each other. As love grows and matures, they find that they don't have to talk quite so much. Somehow they grow together so that they know what the other is thinking without asking. Their love becomes so strong that they do not need words to communicate their deepest emotions. In a way it is like that with God: as we get to know him better and better, we do not need to put our love for him into words and in the silence of our hearts we speak to God and he speaks to us. As a community, we need silent prayer; and as a community we need the occasion to put our love into words and actions in the liturgy. Silent prayer, spoken prayer: both have their part to play in our lives as Christians.

*John Dalrymple, *Costing not less than everything*, Darton, Longman and Todd, 1975.

When Pope Paul VI visited the Holy Land, he stopped in Nazareth and in the course of an address on the Holy Family of Jesus, Mary and Joseph, and their life in Nazareth, he said:

First, we learn from its silence. If only we could once again appreciate its great value. We need this wonderful state of mind, beset as we are by the cacophony of strident protests and conflicting claims so characteristic of these turbulent times. The silence of Nazareth should teach us how to meditate in peace and quiet, to reflect on the deeply spiritual, and to be open to the voice of God's inner wisdom and the counsel of his true teachers. Nazareth can teach us the value of study and preparation, of meditation, of a well-ordered spiritual life, and of silent prayer that is known only to God.

CHAPTER 26

Jesus cares for the sick

I know of an old lady who, for many years, was a daily Mass-goer. Each day of her life she went to Mass and received Jesus in communion. She wasn't too worried or disturbed by the changes in the way the Mass was celebrated, because her faith told her that, whether it was in Latin or in English, it was still the Mass which Jesus had first celebrated and commanded his followers to go on celebrating to the end of time.

Then came a serious illness which confined her to bed and, all of a sudden, daily Mass was gone. Instead, the priest came once a month on the First Friday to bring her communion. He was a busy man with many sick calls to make and he could only spend a few minutes with her. Of course, she used her missal on Sundays and she prayed every day but somehow it wasn't the same. She was to all intents and purposes cut off from her parish, from the community which gathered to worship in church each week.

You will know of such cases in your own parish and it is easy to say that it is not possible for the priests of the parish to do more – many priests in fact manage to visit the sick every week – again usually on a Friday, the day of the Lord's crucifixion. It is on Sunday, however, the most important day of the week, that most sick people feel really cut off from their parish.

Now the Church has always had a great care for the sick, following the example of Jesus himself whose ministry in Galilee had consisted of preaching the Good News and curing those who were ill. There are so many examples in the Gospels that we need have no doubt of Jesus' great love and care for those who were sick.

After his death and resurrection, the Church carried on

this mission and there are several cures recorded in the
Acts of the Apostles, the history of the early Church.

On one occasion when Peter cured a lame man, the
crowds were astonished and came running up, wondering
at what had happened. Peter forcefully explained:

It is the name of Jesus which, through our faith in it, has brought
back the strength of this man you see here and who is well
known to you. It is faith in that name which has restored this
man to health as you can all see (from Acts of the Apostles,
chapter 3).

A little later, we have a description of another cure:

Peter visited one place after another and eventually came to the
saints living down in Lydda. There he found a man called
Aeneas, a paralytic who had been bedridden for eight years.
Peter said to him, 'Aeneas, Jesus Christ cures you: get up and
fold your sleeping mat.' Aeneas got up immediately (from Acts
of the Apostles, chapter 9).

Over the centuries the Church has gone on caring for the
sick. She has prayed over the sick person, anointed him
with oil that he might recover from his illness. She has
brought communion to him and at the last moments of his
life, the priest has been with him to help him make his last
journey through death to the new life of God's kingdom.

The Anointing of the Sick could only be given to a
baptised Christian who had asked forgiveness for his sins
and there was a time in the Church's history when the
penances given to sinners were so severe that they tended
to take a chance and only go to confession on their death
bed. The Rite of Anointing of the sick person was inserted
into this death-bed penance and instead of being a sacrament for the sick it became a sacrament for the dying and
was called the Last Anointing or Extreme Unction. Today
the Church has made it clear that there are rites for the sick
and rites for the dying and that the rites for the sick should
be given when the person is conscious and may benefit
from them. Many people speak of the peace of mind

brought by the Rite of Anointing, and many have recovered or at least improved after being anointed. The anointing is really for more serious illnesses when there is some danger of death or, say, before a surgical operation. Communion should however be brought to the sick frequently and the Church encourages it daily during the Easter season.

Bringing communion to the sick was the original reason for reserving the Blessed Sacrament in the tabernacles of our churches and it was only very much later that people started to pray before the Blessed Sacrament, and to have special services of Exposition and Benediction. Communion of the sick is still the main reason for reserving the sacrament, but, of course, it is right that we should make time to pray there.

How are we to bring communion to the sick frequently, especially with our present shortage of priests? The answer lies in the growth of the numbers of Special Ministers of Communion in our parishes. At present special ministers are used mainly to help in the distribution of communion at Sunday Masses, but an important part of their ministry is to bring communion to the sick. An ideal day for this is Sunday and many parishes have now established the custom of bringing communion to the sick after the Sunday Masses. The special ministers come to the altar after communion and are then given the Blessed Sacrament in a pyx (a small container) which they take to a number of sick people in the parish.

This very giving of the Blessed Sacrament to the ministers is a vivid reminder to the community of their sick brothers and sisters who cannot be there, and must encourage them to pray for them.

When the special minister arrives at the sick person's house, he holds a short communion service which consists of a penitential rite, a reading from scripture (perhaps the Gospel of the day), the Lord's prayer, communion, and a final prayer. The service can be shortened or lengthened depending on the condition of the person who is ill.

Afterwards the minister will have time to chat with the sick person, perhaps giving him the parish newsletter and generally bringing him up to date with parish news and events.

If all sick people are to benefit from this care of the sick, it will be necessary for all parishes to have special ministers. This will, in turn, involve the parish community ever more and more intimately with the care of the sick and must make for a more open, caring and praying parish. When communion is brought to the sick person the knowledge that he is being remembered and prayed for will help him to face his sufferings with faith and courage. At the same time, the reception of communion will remind him of how Christ suffered, and he will be given the grace to unite his sufferings with those of Christ for the good of the other members of the parish. In this way, the sick and healthy members of the parish will be united in a great bond of love.

In holy communion, we meet the same Jesus who went about healing the sick, loving and pitying them. When the sick receive communion the prayers which are said ask for their healing:

> God our Father, almighty and eternal,
> we confidently call upon you
> that the body (and blood) of Christ
> which our brother (sister) has received
> may bring him (her)
> lasting health in mind and body.
>
> We ask this in the name of Jesus the Lord.

The growth and development of the ministry to the sick in the parish can only help our parishes to grow in love. In this ministry we can see Jesus whom we have met in our celebration of Mass, coming out with us to love, comfort and heal those who are sick.

CHAPTER 27

At the hour of our death

If there is one taboo in our society today, it is discussion of death. We rarely speak of it, we try to put death to one side because in an age which sees man as dominating creation, without any need of God, death remains the great mystery, the great challenge to the omnipotence of man, the great leveller. As Woody Allen put it: 'It's not that I'm afraid to die. I just don't want to be there when it happens.'

At the second Vatican Council, the bishops of the world gathered in Rome to set in motion the renewal of the Church which is still going on today. One of the subjects they considered was the question of death and here is how they summarised the present-day attitudes to it:

It is in the face of death that the riddle of human existence becomes more acute. Not only is man tormented by pain and by the advancing deterioration of his body, but even more so by a dread of perpetual extinction. . . . Through Christ and in Christ the riddles of sorrow and death grow meaningful. Apart from his Gospel, they overwhelm us. Christ has risen, destroying death by his death.

As Christians we believe that death is not the end, but really the beginning of a new life with God and all the saints. In the words of one of the Prefaces of Christian Death:

In him who rose from the dead,
our hope of resurrection dawned.
The sadness of death gives way
to the bright promise of immortality.

Lord, for your faithful people, life is changed not ended.
When the body of our earthly dwelling place lies in death,
we gain an everlasting dwelling place in heaven.

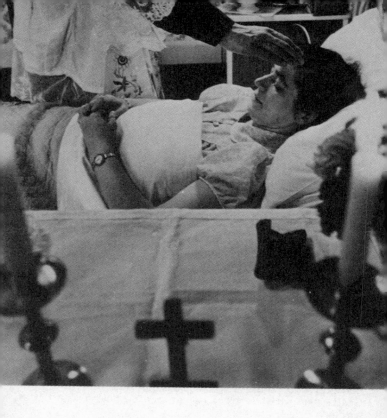

The final blessing shows how closely Jesus is united with the dying person on his last journey

Although the Church in her ministry to the sick prays that the sick will recover, she knows that we must all die one day, and so helps us to prepare for that day. One of the most 'Catholic' of all prayers, the Hail Mary, asks Mary to pray for us 'now and at the hour of our death' and the final official prayer of the Church at the end of the day, Compline, asks 'for a restful night and a perfect death' (ICEL translation).

When a person is seriously ill and death is imminent, the priest is called and will give the dying person *the* Sacrament of the Dying, which is known as Viaticum, which is communion of the sick, but with special prayers. Now, if at all possible, it should be given to the dying person during Mass celebrated at his bedside.

The purpose of this last sacrament is explained in this way:

Before he left this world to return to the Father, our Lord Jesus Christ gave us this sacrament of his body and blood, so that when the hour comes for us to pass from this life to join him, we may be reassured and strengthened by this pledge of our resurrection, this food for our journey, the Lord's own body and blood.

From the time that we were born and baptised, the Eucharist has been with us in all the events of our life. Baptism looks forward to the day when we make our first communion. When we married, our wedding may well have been celebrated during Mass; when we had children they could have been baptised during Mass; when we were ill, we might have had Mass in our homes. In our joys and in our sorrows, the Mass was always there, the centre of our lives, giving us the strength to live as Christ's people and now, at the end, Christ comes to us once more under the forms of bread and wine to accompany us on that final journey through death to our new life, united with God and all the saints in heaven. During the service, the dying person will, if he is able, be asked to renew the promises of his baptism and after he has received communion in the usual way, the priest will say:

> May the Lord Jesus Christ protect you
> and lead you to eternal life.

The final prayer continues this theme:

> Father,
> your Son, Jesus Christ, is our way, our truth, and our life.
> Our brother (sister) . . . entrusts himself (herself) to you
> with full confidence in all your promises.
> Refresh him (her) with the body and blood of your Son
> and lead him (her) to your kingdom in peace.

The final blessing shows how closely Jesus is united with the dying person in his last journey:

> May the Lord Jesus Christ be with you to protect you.
> May he go before you to guide you
> and stand behind you to give you strength.
> May he look upon you to keep you and bless you.

And so at these last moments, Jesus is with the dying person. Even when the priest has gone, the family and friends should continue to pray for and with the dying person, giving him their love and comfort as he prepares to make his last journey.

This is the testing time for our faith: has everything we believed been a lie, a mass of superstitions? Is there really any life beyond the grave? When I die, will I really live again or will I just be nothing? Only faith can now sustain the person on his death bed and the presence and comfort of those he has loved will help him.

Father Michael Hollings in one of the most beautiful books I know, records this incident, and it is a most fitting way to end this chapter.

A dear friend of mine who had married comparatively late in life, had spent much of his life in the Sudan, and had acquired an enlarged heart, and frequent bouts of heart failure. His wife and I and he often prayed together, had Mass in his home, and eventually came to hospital together on a particularly bad heart failure. As he lay in considerable pain in the hospital bed, with myself on one side and his wife on the other, various doctors and nurses were doing all they could to relieve the pain. Then one doctor came to him and said he was going to give him an injection and this would make him better. His reply was straight, simple and moving. He said: 'Don't do that. I want to go to God.' Then he turned his head to his wife and looked lovingly at her and said: 'I love you very much, but I want to go to God.'

He was injected, and he survived a little, so that the two of them spent a night of real joy together in the hospital, while they talked quietly and happily of the past, their life together and their love. When I arrived about six in the morning to see how they were, he had just quietly breathed his last, and I was able to give her communion at his bedside and pray with her. I have never seen such a wonderful mingling of deep sorrow, complete love and from her a real joy that he was now with God to whom he longed to go.*

*Michael Hollings, *Alive to Death, Thoughts on suffering, death and mourning*, Mayhew McCrimmon Ltd, 1976.

CHAPTER 28

The end of the beginning

And so we have come to the end of our journey through the Mass, but I hope that for you it will really be the beginning. In these pages I have tried to show what the Mass means for me. I have tried to avoid abstruse theological explanations and the dreadful jargon which is sometimes prevalent in theological circles.

When Jesus was on earth, he spoke to those who came to him in simple and human terms – not for him the abstractions of theology! For him the kingdom of heaven was a mustard seed, or yeast. God was our Father, our daddy; he was the shepherd who left ninety-nine sheep to go and find one that was lost; he was the woman who had lost a coin and cleaned the whole house until she found it.

Jesus left us the Mass so that we might make present in our own time his life, his death and his resurrection. Of course, there have been changes since his time but at the heart of it all there still remain the bread and the wine which by the power of Jesus' word become his body and blood. In these simple symbols, Jesus reaches out to us in his Church today wishing to unite us ever more closely with himself.

I hope that this book will help the Mass to live for you so that when you go to church next Sunday, some of the things I have written will, by God's grace, help you to deepen your faith and your love for the Mass so that it will really be a meeting with Jesus. In this way the Mass will become the centre of your life, giving you all the courage and the strength that it needs to bear witness to Jesus today.

The Mass is the most important thing that we can do as Christians. It is up to us to show in our lives that it really matters to us.

The Mass is ended, all go in peace.
We must diminish,
    and Christ increase.
We take him with us
    where'er we go
that through our actions
    his life may show.*

*Sebastian Temple